NEW BEGINNINGS

SKILLS FOR SINGLE PARENTS AND STEPFAMILY PARENTS

PARENT'S MANUAL

Don Dinkmeyer,
Gary D. McKay, and
Joyce L. McKay

RESEARCH PRESS
2612 North Mattis Avenue
Champaign, Illinois 61821

To my grandchildren and stepgrandchildren, Drew, Caitlin, Luke, and Joshua, who each provided a new beginning.
Don Dinkmeyer

To Rob, Joyce's son and Gary's stepson, for his continuing interest in and support of our work.
Joyce and Gary McKay

Contents

List of Charts

Acknowledgments

Our approach to parenting has been presented in a number of publications, most notably *Systematic Training for Effective Parenting* published by American Guidance Service in 1976. In *New Beginnings* we turn to the unique challenges facing single parents and stepfamily parents. Many people were involved in helping us develop this material and we wish to acknowledge them with fondest appreciation—

All the single parents and stepfamily parents we've known and worked with over the years.

E. Jane Dinkmeyer, Nancy Richards, and Norma Stevens, who went the extra mile in typing, collating, mailing, retyping, and photocopying to help us bring *New Beginnings* into existence.

Emily Visher and John Visher, renowned authors and authorities on stepfamilies, who gave their time and effort in reviewing this material.

A very special thanks to E. Jane Dinkmeyer for her patience and continuing encouragement.

Jackie Wessel, sister and sister-in-law of Joyce and Gary McKay, whose model helped us learn more about being an effective single parent.

A special appreciation to Mary Wolf for her careful editing and attention to detail and to Ann Wendel, president of Research Press, for her support and enthusiasm. Thanks also to Bob Lange, Claire Chapdu, Russ Pence, Dennis Wiziecki, and the rest of the Research Press staff.

The late Rudolf Dreikurs, who taught us the applications of Adlerian psychology to parent-child relationships.

Dear Parent:

You may be wondering, "Why a book and program for both single parents and stepfamily parents? Aren't these families distinctly different?" While there are differences in these family structures, there are also many important similarities that you will be learning about. Single parents and stepfamily parents have a lot in common and can learn from each other's experiences. Many stepparents know what it's like to be single parents. Single parents often remarry and become members of a stepfamily. Regardless of your family structure, there is much you can learn about your family and about effective parenting skills in *New Beginnings*.

In the eight chapters in *New Beginnings*, you will learn about building your family's self-esteem, communicating and solving problems more effectively, disciplining democratically, and many other parenting skills and concepts. You may wish to go through the book on your own or you may want to join a *New Beginnings* parent group.

The changes you will be asked to make in *New Beginnings* will not always be easy. But the rewards of your new beliefs and skills are worth every effort. You can learn to turn any obstacles you see in your family structure into opportunities.

New Beginnings is written by three people who understand your situation. They are all members of stepfamilies as either a biological parent, stepparent, or stepgrandparent. One was a single parent. They have all experienced the emotional pain you may be struggling with as a single parent or stepfamily parent. But they have also experienced the joy of membership in their new families. Through hard work and commitment, they have made their relationships effective—they have made a new beginning and you can too!

Chapter 1

Issues in Single Parenting and Stepfamily Parenting

Janna has been divorced for less than a year. She finds that the stress of providing for her children on her salary as a secretary, handling all of the discipline problems, and losing most of the friends who supported her when she was married leaves her angry and tired most of the time. Her 10-year-old, Ryan, is always testing her authority through angry shouting matches. Her 7-year-old, Kim, who was independent and mature before Janna's divorce, clings and whines. Bruce, Janna's ex-spouse, does not help Janna in her attempts to deal with the children. When he has the children he encourages them to do things that Janna does not allow. Janna is still quite hurt about their divorce and finds herself unable to speak civilly to Bruce at this time.

Peter expected to have a big, happy family when he married Marie and their two families moved in together. Instead, he found that almost everyone involved was angry and bitter. His two girls do not accept Marie as their mother, and Marie's three children do not accept Peter as their father. All of the children bicker almost constantly over privileges and possessions. Although the bond between Peter and Marie is strong, they feel it beginning to weaken because of the children's hostility and the lack of support they receive from their relatives and the community.

As a single parent or stepparent, you probably have experienced problems similar to Janna's or Peter's. In addition to the usual child-rearing problems that all parents face, single parents and stepfamily parents face some unique problems because of their family structures. This does not mean that single-parent families or stepfamilies are somehow not as good as the traditional nuclear family (two biological parents and their chil-

1

dren). Single-parent families and stepfamilies have some different weaknesses than traditional families, but they also have some different strengths. This book will help you explore the weaknesses and strengths in your family and solve those problems resulting from your family structure and those problems common to all kinds of families. You will begin in this chapter by learning about the similarities and differences between single-parent families and stepfamilies and the expectations parents and the community may have about both types of family.

Similarities of Single-Parent Families and Stepfamilies

By the end of the twentieth century, single-parent families and stepfamilies will outnumber traditional nuclear families in the United States. In 1985, there were 1.2 million divorces.[1] Almost 75 percent of the people who divorce will remarry, and many of these remarriages will involve stepchildren.[2] The number of parents who have never been married or who choose to remain single after divorce is also increasing. These single-parent families and stepfamilies are much more similar to each other than they are to traditional nuclear families.

Most single-parent families and stepfamilies have suffered the loss of a primary relationship and are missing a biological parent. When the separation and loss is because of death or divorce, family members feel grief and pain and must go through the grieving process before the family can begin to work as a new unit. The absent biological parent continues to play an important part in the family structure—whether the parent is dead or alive.[3] In both family structures, there may be an ex-spouse to deal with in matters involving the children. Even though a spouse and extended family members may be "ex" to an adult, they are not "ex" to the children. Creative planning is often required on holidays and special occasions to allow children time with both parents and their families.

Children in single-parent families and stepfamilies may be members of more than one household with very different rules and values. Altering behavior and perceptions to accommodate both households is a continuing source of stress for all family members.

Financial problems are one of the greatest sources of stress for both single-parent families and stepfamilies. Children of divorce living with women who are single parents are the fastest growing segment of American poor.[4] Many women suddenly faced with the need to earn an adequate income find they lack the skills or opportunities to do so. Both single parents and stepparents often have to contribute to the support of more than one household. The incomes that supported one household may not stretch to cover two.

Society views both the single-parent family and the stepfamily as nonstandard. Both groups often feel they must work harder to be more like the traditional family. They may see their problems as a result of not belonging to a traditional nuclear family. The multiple roles required of single parents and stepparents are largely ignored, misunderstood, and criticized by society. These parents receive little support or encouragement from the community, schools, churches, public agencies, and public policy-makers. This results in greatly increased stress on the family.

The Uniqueness of Each Family Structure

Although single-parent families and stepfamilies share many similarities, they each have some characteristics that are unique to their individual structures. The most basic difference between these families is the number of adults in the home. By definition, single-parent families usually have only one adult in the home. Society often blames the misbehavior of children from single-parent families on the fact that these children do not have adult role models of both sexes living with them. Stepfamilies have an adult couple in the household. Society often views them as nuclear families and expects them to function as such. Unfortunately, many stepfamilies accept this view and set unreasonably high expectations. If they cannot meet these expectations, they feel like failures and perceive themselves as inferior rather than just different.

In single-parent families, both biological parents have an established relationship to the children. In stepfamilies, on the other hand, there is an established relationship developed in a previous family structure between only one of the adults and the children.

The extended family network in stepfamilies may be much larger and more complex than in a single-parent family. When a biological parent remarries, the parent's children acquire not only a stepparent but also the new stepparent's extended family.

Changes in the Nuclear Family

Changes in the family have not been restricted to new types of family structures. Social and economic changes have altered the roles of all family members. Society, in general, has moved away from an autocratic system (based on relationships between superiors and inferiors and using punishment and reward) toward a more democratic system (based on social equality and rights and responsibilities). The family, too, has moved away from an autocratic system, based on the parents' (particularly the father's) authority and the children's obedience, toward a more democratic ideal of mutual respect and responsibility.

The role of women in the family may have changed most drastically. Many middle-class women entered the work force for the first time during World War II, when they were needed to replace men. At the end of the war, some of these women were not willing to return to the role of full-time homemaker, and families came to enjoy the benefits of two incomes. The civil rights movement of the 1960s and the feminist movement led more women to enter the work force. Inflation and the changing economy of the 1970s, which left many families unable to meet their basic needs on one income, also increased the number of women working outside the home.

An increasing focus on women's rights and equality has made many women no longer willing to work just for money in low-paying jobs. Women are looking at career options and opportunities. With career training and advancement, women have increased their ability to be in charge of their own lives.

Equality at home also has become an issue. Many women push for changes in traditional male and female family roles and attempt to get their husbands and children to share in the household tasks. This sharing of tasks puts stress on some families but also has benefits. Families who share household tasks have time for other activities together and learn how to function as a cooperative unit. Unless they learn to enlist cooperation from family members, women who find themselves in full-time career and homemaker roles may suffer from burnout and other stress-related illnesses.

Couples now often delay marriage and beginning a family until their late twenties or early thirties in order to establish their careers and to build their relationship without children. Financial independence for women has led many couples to expect more personal satisfaction from their relationships. Therefore, dissatisfaction with the marriage relationship has increased the number of couples seeking divorce as a solution to marital problems.

With the increase in families in which both parents work outside the home has come a change in childcare. The number of latchkey children and children in day-care centers has increased. The role of children has also changed in some families, with children expected to be more responsible for their own care.

In spite of all of these changes, the myth of the nuclear family has remained intact. Society still sees the family as being composed of a mother and father and their 2.5 biological children. Father is still often seen as earning the money and Mother as taking care of the home and children. That description doesn't fit most of today's families, but is still used as a measure of normality. Much of the stress currently experienced by all families is related to acceptance of this myth as the goal to be attained and feelings of failure when it isn't reached.

Unrealistic Community Myths and Expectations

Change is difficult. When a great deal of change occurs quickly in a basic institution like the family, society initially deals with it by trying to make the new structure fit the old definitions. The easiest way to do this is by developing stereotypes.

Society often assumes "normal" is what has been and "abnormal" is that which is different. Many of the unrealistic expectations placed on single-parent families and stepfamilies by the community are based on society's acceptance of the myth of the nuclear family as a standard for all families.

Single Parents

One societal misconception is that children must have both a full-time mother and father in the home to grow up mentally healthy. The implication is that children will not be mentally healthy if they have only one full-time parent. But research shows that a far greater chance for children to develop unhealthy perceptions exists in families where there is frequent fighting between parents who stay together just for the sake of the children than in single-parent families.[5]

Another mistaken belief is that children's behavior problems are solely the result of divorce. Single-parent families have the ability to transmit all the components of mutual respect and caring basic to the healthy social and emotional growth of family members. However, it is apparent that attention frequently has been focused on the negative behavioral and emotional consequences of divorce and separation.[6]

Regardless of their family structure, children's behavior often changes temporarily when there are changes in the family. Any kind of shift in the family pattern, such as a move, job change, new baby, illness, or loss of a family member, may result in behavior problems as the children adjust to new situations. The temporary problems only become permanent if they are reinforced.

Stepparents

A typical stepfamily may include two stepparents, two sets of stepchildren, ex-spouses and their new families, and all the extended family members related to these groups. Success of the stepfamily is largely determined by the ability of the two separate families to cooperate.[7]

Books, movies, and television provide many different models of stepfamilies. Many of these models portray the stereotype of either the instantly loving family with no problems or the wicked stepparent and miserable stepchildren. Both portrayals are inaccurate.

Expecting stepfamilies to function just like nuclear families is unrealistic. Love does not occur instantly in stepfamilies and family relationships must be built up slowly.

Portraying stepparents as cruel and uncaring toward their stepchildren is also unrealistic and harmful. Many people get their idea of stepmothers from the fairy tale "Cinderella," in which the stepmother is mean, stingy, manipulative, unloving, and favors her own children. Considering the large number of stepmothers in the population, it is unfortunate for stepfamilies that this negative stereotype still exists.[8] Stepfathers, too, are often portrayed as cruel and unloving. These portrayals encourage the myth that stepfamilies are bad places to rear children. Stepmothers are seen as mean and ugly, stepfathers as cold and harsh, and stepchildren as pitiful wretches.[9]

Society needs to replace fairy tales with reality. Stepfamilies have their own set of challenges and rewards and are no better or worse than other families—just different. The following chart will summarize for you some of the myths and realities of single-parent families and stepfamilies.

Unrealistic Parental Expectations

Unrealistic parental expectations often come from a parent's believing that to develop normally children must grow up in a family like the mythical nuclear family. Single parents and stepparents who try to make their families like nuclear families usually only succeed in feeling guilty and discounting the positive aspects of their own families. Realistic expectations for single-parent families and stepfamilies are those that are achievable, reasonable, and fit the family structure. Achievable expectations encourage both parents and children and help the new family grow.

Chart 1. Myths and Realities of
Single-Parent Families and Stepfamilies

Myth	*Reality*
Nuclear families are the "normal" type of family.	By the end of the twentieth century, single-parent families and stepfamilies will outnumber nuclear families.
Single-parent families and stepfamilies have little in common.	Single-parent families and stepfamilies are more like each other then they are like nuclear families. • Both are families born of loss. • Both may have ex-spouses and children who live in two households. • Both may face financial problems. • Both are seen as nonstandard by society.
Children must have both a full-time mother and father in the home to grow up mentally healthy.	Children are more likely to develop problems in a home where parents fight frequently than in a home with a loving single parent.
Children whose parents are divorced can be expected to suffer behavior problems and problems in school.	Any change in the family structure can result in temporary behavior problems. These problems only become permanent when they are reinforced.
Stepfamilies are just like nuclear families.	Love does not occur instantly in stepfamilies and family relationships must be built up slowly.
Stepparents are cruel and uncaring toward their stepchildren.	Most stepparents care for their stepchildren and are concerned for their welfare.

Single Parents

The unrealistic expectation "I must be both mother and father" is a major source of stress for many single parents. One significant, caring adult can help a child develop into a responsible, psychologically healthy person. Although it is true that it is helpful for a child to have a close relationship with a role model of the same sex as the absent parent, this role model can be provided in a variety of ways. Extended family members, friends, members of organizations like Big Brothers and Big Sisters, and counselors or teachers are some examples of role models available to children from single-parent families.

Some single parents believe they must be "superparents" in order to prove they are adequate. Parents who choose this role think they must show the world that their children will not miss out on anything because there is only one parent in the home. To prove they are adequate, they tend to say yes to requests that they would have refused if they were a parent in a nuclear family.

> Kitty is a single parent with two girls in grade school. Since her divorce, she has returned to full-time work as a computer programmer. Even though she is now working full time and has very little time to spare, she feels she must continue with the volunteer activities she did for the school before her divorce. She sews costumes for the school play, bakes cookies for the classroom for special occasions, and attends PTA meetings. She also feels that she must take on new challenges to show what a good parent she is. Recently she volunteered to lead one daughter's Girl Scout troop and coach the other daughter's softball team.

Such parents are frequently overwhelmed and overburdened. They suffer from chronic fatigue and a feeling of inadequacy. In trying to please everybody, they please nobody.

Finally, some single parents believe they must make it up to the children for the divorce. They assume the responsibility for putting their children in a "disadvantaged" status and feel sorry for them. They tend to overprotect, discipline inconsistently, encourage materialism, and feel guilty when they have to say no.

Stepparents

New stepfamilies do not come equipped with a guarantee of instant love from the stepchildren. Stepparents who expect that being in love with a new spouse ensures love from that person's children are setting themselves up for disappointment.

Many stepparents want to try to become a parent, attempting to replace the absent biological parent; however, most stepchildren are unwilling to accept the new stepparent as a parent just because their mother or father has married this person. The children have a biological parent elsewhere to whom they feel this love belongs. It is up to the stepparents in these families to prove themselves.

Stepparents who do not demand instant love have a better chance of eventually winning over the children. Working to attain the children's respect and acceptance is the best way to build a relationship. The children can accept this as a way to relate to the stepparent without being disloyal to their biological parent. The unrealistic beliefs of stepparents and single parents will be discussed in more detail in Chapter 2.

The Bond of Pre-existing Relationships

Both single parents and stepparents may misunderstand the continuing bond between children and their other biological parent. The original parent-child bond continues to exist after divorce even if the children form new bonds. Therefore, if at all possible, it is important for children to maintain a relationship with the other biological parent. Stepparents and single parents who keep the following facts in mind will be better equipped to meet the challenges of their new role.

1. The bond of pre-existing relationships will not stop with formation of the new family.
2. The bond between biological parents and their children will continue to exist—even if the parent is dead.
3. Any attempt to interfere with the original parent-child bond will be met with hostility and will create problems.
4. Biological parents will at times favor their children over their spouse and stepchildren.
5. The parent-child bond in single-parent homes becomes stronger each year the parent remains single. After several years, it may be more difficult for a stepparent to be accepted into the family.
6. Stepparents cannot replace the biological parent but must establish a new stepparent-stepchild bond.

"Can I get you a stamp for that letter?"

Building Understanding of Different Family Structures

Many of the difficulties experienced in single-parent families or stepfamilies are the same as those found in traditional nuclear families. Disagreements between parent and child, competition between siblings, discipline problems, children looking for a "second opinion" when one parent has said no, and lack of support from members of the extended family are familiar themes heard from all parents— regardless of their family structure.

Accepting society's view of the single-parent family or stepfamily as substandard allows the parents to blame child-rearing problems on the family structure. It is true that the degree of some problems may temporarily be affected by the family structure. However, when parents believe the "myth of the nuclear family" and use it to measure their parental effectiveness, they will feel discouraged and will reduce their ability to deal with the situation. By accepting society's mistaken belief, they reinforce it and devalue their own family structure. Here's an example of a school conference to illustrate this point.

> Sandy is a fifth-grade student who has been a bright, cheerful achiever but is not doing as well this year. The teacher calls Sandy's mother, Debbie, to come in for a conference. During the conference in an attempt to pinpoint the problem, the teacher asks, "Is anything different at home?" Debbie answers, "Yes, there is. Sandy's father and I were divorced last summer." The teacher nods her head knowingly, believing that she has found the answer to Sandy's poor performance, and she unconsciously lowers her expectations for improvement. She believes the myth that divorce produces poor school performance.

How might the teacher have reacted if Sandy were not from a single-parent family? In the next example, Jim, who is from a nuclear family, is having trouble in school.

> During the conference with Jim's mother, Marta, when the teacher asks, "Is anything different at home?" she gets the following response: "Not really, except Jim's dad is traveling more in

his new job. Could that be the reason?" The teacher sees Jim's behavior as a temporary reaction to the situation and continues to explore alternatives with Marta. The conference ends with the teacher saying, "Let's wait and see. I'm sure Jim will adjust to this and get back on track."

Both examples are similar in nature—a temporary setback in the forward progress of a bright, achieving child. However, in the first example both the teacher and the mother see Sandy as the victim of an abnormal situation. In the second example, Jim's problem is seen as a temporary reaction to a normal family situation. The teachers' expectations may have an influence on both students' performance during the rest of the school year.

Sandy's mother can keep this temporary setback from becoming a permanent roadblock if she refuses to accept her single-parent status as the cause of the problem. She can educate the teacher on how expectations can become self-fulfilling prophecies and on the potential damage done to children by accepting the myth that single-parent families are substandard. At the same time, the mother can work with Sandy by providing encouragement and listening to her concerns.

In the second example, there is no guarantee Jim will adjust and get back on track simply because the teacher thinks he will. Although her expectations may provide some encouragement, Jim's parents will also need to assess what they can do differently at home.

Until now you may have accepted without question some of the myths about family structure making a family a good or bad place to raise children and, thus, felt discouraged about your own family. As this chapter has shown you, all kinds of families face problems and all families have different strengths to solve their problems. If you believe in the strength of your family, you can face any situation and make it better. Building your self-esteem and your children's self-esteem, as you will see next, is the first step to solving family problems.

Activity Assignment

During the next week, ask each person in your family to identify one thing about the family the person feels good about. Post the list of good feelings where everyone in the family can see it. If any children are too young to read and write, they can draw pictures to show their good feelings.

Important Points to Remember in Chapter 1

1. Single-parent families and stepfamilies will outnumber nuclear families by the end of the twentieth century.

2. Single-parent families and stepfamilies have more in common with each other than they do with traditional nuclear families. Some of the ways in which single-parent families and stepfamilies are similar include:

- Both are families born of loss.
- Both may have ex-spouses and children who live in two households.
- Both may face financial problems.
- Both are seen as nonstandard by society.

3. Some of the ways in which single-parent families and stepfamilies are different include:

- Each has a different number of adults in the household.
- All relationships among family members are not yet established in the stepfamily.
- The extended family of stepfamilies is larger.

4. Societal and economic changes, such as the change from an autocratic to a more democratic society and changing male and female roles, have affected family life.

5. The community holds some unrealistic expectations of single-parent families and stepfamilies including:

- Children must have both a full-time mother and a full-time father to grow up mentally healthy.
- Behavior problems are solely the result of divorce.
- Stepfamilies are just like nuclear families.
- Stepparents are cruel and unloving to their stepchildren.

6. Single parents and stepparents hold some unreasonable expectations including:

- "I must be both mother and father to my children."

- "I must be a superparent."
- "I must make it up to my children for the divorce."
- "I must get instant love from my stepchildren."

7. Realistic expectations for single parents and stepfamily parents are those that are achievable, reasonable, and fit the family structure.

8. Children don't divorce their parents. There will be a continuing relationship between a child and the other biological parent.

9. Accepting the "myth of the nuclear family" is discouraging to single parents and stepfamily parents and reduces their ability to deal with their problems.

Chapter 2

Self-Esteem

Does being a single parent or a stepparent reduce your self-esteem? Certainly, when people move into a new situation they may feel a reduction in self-esteem and confidence. But it is best to look at the self-esteem as temporarily misplaced—not lost. The meaning that you give to your new status as a single parent or stepparent influences your self-esteem and confidence.

> Beth has always been a confident person and sure of herself as a parent. However, her divorce seems to have had an effect upon her self-confidence. She doesn't feel that people treat her the same as a single person. The activities that she used to enjoy, such as going to church and going out with other couples, do not feel the same, and she does not think that she fits in the way she did before. She feels uncomfortable and uncertain about herself.

If Beth can think of herself as capable, confident, and socially acceptable, as she did before her divorce, then the change in her status will not necessarily affect her self-esteem. *The meaning we give to a situation, not the situation itself, influences our self-esteem and self-confidence.* You had the capacity to develop your self-esteem and self-confidence before your change in marital status, and the change in status in itself does not necessarily lower your self-esteem or your capacity to develop self-esteem, although you may experience a temporary lack of confidence.

Self-esteem is your inner confidence and feelings of self-worth that allow you to feel positive about yourself. These feelings are based upon unconditional self-acceptance and self-respect. Self-esteem builds from within. It is not based upon what others think about you but upon recognition of and acceptance of all your resources, talents, strengths, and contributions. Self-esteem also includes accepting your mistakes, limitations, and basic human imperfections and not allowing these to keep you from feeling lovable and capable.[1] For adults and children, self-esteem is the root of all happiness and effectiveness in life. Self-esteem is important in all areas of life. Certainly the way that you feel about yourself affects the way in which you relate to other people. Low self-esteem makes it difficult to meet the challenges of living.

In this chapter, you will learn to enhance your self-esteem through self-encouragement and changing your discouraging beliefs. You will also learn the difference between praise and encouragement and how to build your children's self-esteem through encouragement.

Encouragement and Discouragement

Encouragement involves focusing on an individual's resources in order to build that person's self-esteem, self-confidence, and feelings of worth. When you encourage, you focus on any resource that can be turned into an asset or strength.[2] People who encourage are able to see what is positive in any interaction. Instead of being negative, critical, and looking for weaknesses and faults, they see the positive side in themselves, others, and the challenges life presents.

Often a change in family structure initially creates a discouraging situation. However, in any discouraging situation, there is the potential for encouragement. You need to look at whatever has happened and identify the positive possibilities in the situation.

Discouragement occurs when you believe you are inadequate or feel that you cannot meet the standards you or others have set. If you are discouraged, you may give up. People who are discouraged may still seek recognition and strive to be successful as other people do. However, they have learned ineffective ways of reaching their goals. They use these ineffective techniques because they believe these are the only ways they can get what they want.

Self-Encouragement

You give yourself feelings of worth and value. This is best done by learning to build a positive relationship with yourself. Ask yourself these questions: "Do I treat myself as I treat a friend? Am I respectful of my needs and my desires? Do I take care of myself? Do I spend some time alone and pursue my hobbies? Do I exercise, eat right, and get enough rest?" Your answers to these questions will tell you what kind of a relationship you have with yourself.

It is important as a single parent to reach out and make new friends. Single parents quickly learn that they are not going to fit in as easily as before with groups of couples. Former friends may no longer be available since they tend to side with one of the divorced spouses or don't want to show favoritism and avoid both. Some couples may view the single parent as a threat to their marriage. The ex-spouse's parents may no longer be available for support, and sometimes the person's own parents may not accept the situation or be supportive. Single parents need to review and become involved in developing their own skills, interests, and hobbies. Stepparents, too, need to maintain interests and hobbies that they had before joining their new family.

Remember that you may be in a new situation. The decisions that you make may be the ones that are right for you at this point in time, no matter what anyone else thinks. Expect to make some mistakes and handle some things poorly. As you develop a positive relationship with yourself, you will be able to encourage yourself and enhance your self-esteem. If you feel positive and encouraged about yourself, it is likely that you will be able to encourage the rest of your family.

Self-Valuing Statements
Self-valuing statements are important in developing self-esteem. Your language and the way you think directs the way you feel and relate to others. When you make a self-valuing statement, you do not compare yourself to other people or say how much

better you are than somebody else. Self-valuing statements point out your resources and assets without making comparisons. They enable you to value yourself just as you are, even with imperfections.

At times you may have criticized yourself about something you did by thinking, "That was stupid. Nobody with any sense would have done that." You need to recognize that your decisions will not always be correct and that you don't always have to be right to be a worthwhile person. You need to develop self-valuing statements that counteract your criticisms of yourself. These are statements you make to yourself when you are sitting quietly, contemplating, and are accepting of positive thoughts. When these statements have been established in your thoughts, they can be used at other times to replace negative, self-critical thoughts.

Self-valuing statements will always fit the individual, not the world at large. Thus, it is difficult to suggest self-valuing statements for you. Here are some self-valuing statements that other people have made.

"I like the way I'm independent."
"I think for myself."
"I can be counted on."
"I find many ways to look at a situation."
"I'm a good friend."
"People can trust me."

Perhaps these statements fit you. List some other statements here that describe your positive qualities.

_____

_____

_____

_____

Changing Your Discouraging Beliefs

You may believe certain things that discourage you and affect your self-esteem. Some of the common discouraging beliefs of single parents and stepfamily parents and ways to counteract them follow.

1. *I must be in control and my children should not challenge me.* Stepparents who believe they must be in control and should not be challenged set themselves up for defeat. In the same way, when single parents decide to become more controlling because they feel that as the only parent at home they must take charge, they, too, are set up for a challenge from the children. It is only through giving children power and responsibility that parents can reach their real goal—the development of self-control by the children. Instead of trying to control children, parents reduce resistance by empowering children. Giving children choices and responsibility develops self-control.

2. *The children should and must love me.* Single parents who take on full responsibility for the care of the children may feel entitled to love. They may think, "Since I'm taking on all of this responsibility and doing all of this for the children (perhaps working during the day, painting the house at night, and giving up friendships), then the least the children can do is show a lot

of love and be cooperative." When the children are not loving and cooperative, the parent is very discouraged.

The possibilities for discouragement in the stepfamily may be even greater. Stepparents often feel they are making a special effort to deal with children who are not even their legal responsibility. They may feel that the least the children can do is show love and respect. When this does not happen, stepparents may feel, "It's not worth it. Why try?"

Parents must recognize that they can't demand love from their children. Children decide whether or not to love their parents, and their decision does not make the parents any less loveable. Parents can only continue to be positive and caring. It is impossible to control another person's feelings.

3. *I should be treated fairly.* Parents often feel they are being treated unfairly when they believe they are putting a lot of time and effort into the family and at the same time feel a lack of respect from the children. The parents' first impulse may be to try to get even. This often leads the children to feel treated unfairly and to seek revenge, beginning the cycle anew.

Parents who feel they are being treated unfairly must recognize that life ofen *is* unfair and that all of their efforts, intentions, and involvement cannot make it fair. By accepting the unfairness of life, they will be less disturbed if their children treat them in a way that they feel is unfair.

4. *I know what is best.* The belief "I know what is best" is especially common in stepfamilies. Both stepfamily parents tend to believe that the way they did things in their own families is the best way. Neither of them may accept, or even understand, the other's way of behaving.

It's not as important to decide who is right as it is to recognize that different people do things in different ways and need to be accepted in terms of their uniqueness. In stepfamilies, the couple needs to learn to support each other in the relationships with children. However, different families always have different values or opinions and may introduce to each other new ideas about recreation, religion, study habits, table manners, closeness to extended family, and so on. This gives children in step-

"Helen and I accept each other's different ideas, and
she loves to picnic."

families an introduction to the many varied ways of looking at
certain situations and encourages flexibility.

5. *I must replace the absent parent.* No one can expect to
be a replacement for another person. Single parents who try to
be both mother and father find themselves exhausted and discouraged, failing at both jobs. Stepparents who try to replace the
absent parent by competing or being similar to that person will
not win the love of the children. The sooner parents stop trying
to fulfill both parenting roles or meet the standards of an absent
person, the sooner they will be accepted for themselves.

6. *I must make it up to the children for their having only
one parent at home.* Parents may try to make up for a missing
parent by indulging, pitying, and feeling sorry for their children.
These behaviors hinder the children's development of self-
esteem and self-worth. Instead, permit and encourage the children to play an essential part in helping the family function.

Some parents try to make up for the loss of a spouse by being a "superparent," devoting all of their time to their children. It is far more important for both parents and children to reach out and make new friends. This helps parents to develop perspective on life and makes them more effective.

7. *My divorce is a personal failure.* Some people look at divorce as if it were a personal failure. This is where being able to see the positive in a situation can be helpful. Divorce may be an effective solution to a relationship that was not working. Although children may lose a father or mother as a permanent part of the household, they will be freed from most clashes and conflicts.

The new situation is an opportunity, not an obstacle. Single parents are free to convey their own values and opinions to their children. There is now *one* opinion in the household, and children are not pulled, as they may have been previously, between different opinions. Custodial and noncustodial parents are free to convey their values without the usual conflict and disagreement that occurs when two parents inhabiting the same house fight over how to discipline. The children learn to deal in a different way with each parent, accepting the opinion of the parent who is in charge of them at the time instead of seeking another opinion.

8. *My family must prove its worth to the community.* Parents who are overly concerned with prestige, doing well, and having children who are first in the class or outstanding in music or athletics will be disappointed when either they or the children do not meet these expectations. Both single parents and stepfamily parents may tend to look at their children's achievements and behavior as a special indication of the work that they have put into parenting. This view is often formed in response to discouraging community expectations. Parents may adopt an "I'll show you" attitude rather than accepting that they are good enough already. This overambition clearly communicates the message "be more" to the children. Parents seem to vow to show the world how worthwhile their family is. Children under such extreme pressure to succeed tend to have a discouraged outlook upon life.

To reduce their overambition, parents may wish to examine their beliefs and why it is so important to them to live up to other people's standards. Parents may also decide to stop pushing their children to succeed in order to impress others and concentrate instead on building children's self-esteem.

The Courage to Be Imperfect

Perfectionism is very discouraging to the perfectionist and to others. People who are perfectionists assume that they are only worthwhile when they do everything perfectly. Since this is an impossible standard to live up to, they continually set themselves up for discouragement. The price paid for perfectionism is stifled creativity and a fear of making mistakes. Perfectionists are often afraid to take a chance—even though by doing so they may achieve a desired outcome.

If you are to be effective as a human being and as a parent, you need to develop the courage to be imperfect. "The courage to be imperfect" is a phrase attributed to a psychiatrist, Rudolf Dreikurs.[3] Trying to be perfect will leave you permanently dissatisfied and will plague you in all of your relationships.

Are you someone who tries to be perfect? You can evaluate how much you pursue perfection by asking yourself the following questions.

1. Do I feel best when I'm attempting to be perfect?
2. Do I get my best feelings about myself when I compare myself to others and decide that I am better than they are?
3. Are mistakes something that I avoid diligently, often not trying because I would rather not try than fail?
4. Do I see mistakes as dangerous instead of as guides to learning?

Parenting requires creativity, flexibility, and the willingness to take a chance on making mistakes. Each day, parents are presented with new challenges. Perfectionism limits people's ability to see these challenges as opportunities and to explore alternatives. Accepting yourself as adequate to do the job of parenting and deciding that you are doing the best possible job given the resources at hand is a big step forward.

Children tend to view adults as people who never make mistakes. They see adults easily handling apparently difficult tasks and become discouraged and afraid to try because they know they can't perform perfectly. What they don't see is how many attempts it took for the adult to get it right. One of the greatest gifts you can give your children is the courage to be imperfect. Encourage their efforts by letting them see that you also make mistakes. Show them how you learn from mistakes and have the courage to try again.

> Emmie won some money in a contest and immediately went out and bought a washer and dryer. She had wanted a washer and dryer for a long time but could not afford to purchase them. Two weeks after she bought the appliances, Emmie saw the same washer and dryer at another store priced $100 less. Emmie felt terrible about buying the appliances so hastily without comparison shopping and spending the extra $100. She explained to her children the mistake she had made and said that from now on they would all practice comparison shopping, especially on expensive items.

The courage to be imperfect gives you the freedom to try things without fear of failure because you realize that mistakes are part of living. You can become less concerned about status and more concerned about helping and contributing. The only thing that counts after making a mistake is what you do next. Thus, mistakes are not limiters, but they are ways to stretch your potential.

Encouraging Your Children

After you have learned to encourage yourself, you can learn to encourage your children. The opportunities for encouragement in relationships with children are countless. Encouragement improves the relationship between parents and children and increases the cooperation in the family. Children who are encouraged develop confidence, self-reliance, and the ability to face challenges. To encourage a child, you:

1. Look for the positive, emphasizing anything that even has the potential to be positive.
2. Turn negative situations into opportunities for growth.
3. Work with the child by demonstrating cooperation, rather than demanding cooperation.
4. Help the child develop goals the child values.
5. Show confidence.
6. Help the child accept and learn from mistakes.
7. Work to increase the child's self-confidence and courage.

Many people lack the skills to encourage others, but these skills can be learned. The skills, which follow, are within the grasp of each parent.

Listening
Most parents insist, even demand, that their children listen and pay attention to them. Although they make this demand, they

are not necessarily dedicated to listening to their children. Often parents intend to listen to their children but have ineffective skills.

An effective listener is able to thoroughly understand the other person's world, feelings, and beliefs. Effective listeners become involved in and committed to understanding others.

Think of the last time that you were talking with a child. Were you fully attentive to what the child had to say, or did you look in a different direction? Were you distracted? Did you start to think of something "important" you had to do? Did you switch the topic so that you could talk about something that was important to you? Check yourself when you are talking to others. Do you regularly listen closely to others' conversation and follow the feelings and beliefs being expressed?

Think for a moment about your feelings when you are attempting to talk about something important to you and you are aware that the listener is already distracted and off in another world. Listening is a challenging task, but once you learn to do it, it produces results. To listen effectively, you need to:

1. Make direct eye contact. Look at the speaker but do not stare.
2. Be present through your body language. Lean forward and look interested. Make certain the speaker cannot mistake that you are listening.
3. Identify the theme of the person speaking. Be prepared to indicate what you have heard.
4. Pay close attention to the words and to the feelings expressed verbally and nonverbally. Then indicate the feelings you hear. Observe, listen to, and react to any nonverbal communication, such as a facial expression or tone of voice that seemed to show something that the speaker did not say.

Use these guidelines to help encourage your children through listening. You will learn more about listening in Chapter 5, Communication Skills.

Responding to Feelings

Many feelings are expressed in the communication within a family. Feelings give energy to a conversation and make clear to all the primary concerns of the family. But too often family members believe that their feelings are being ignored or criticized and no longer want to bring them up in conversation.

It is important to learn how to respond to the feelings children express. Make certain a child knows that he has been heard and understood, and that you are not criticizing the feelings you hear. Put yourself into the child's world and see things from the child's point of view. Try to understand the feelings so clearly that what you state expresses clearly what the child feels. Recognize that what the child believes and thinks is more important than your interpretation of these beliefs or feelings. Stay with the topic, give your attention, and try to make contact with the child. Chapter 5 will present more specific ideas on how to respond to feelings.

Focusing on Strengths, Efforts, and Contributions

Often parents are quickly able to identify faults and mistakes. Faultfinding, unfortunately, can only lead to poor relationships. You need to look for your children's assets, strengths, and resources and then regularly encourage them. Look for anything positive a child is doing. It may be a very simple kind of contribution, interest, or involvement. Once you have identified the positive action, it is essential to recognize and support it.

> Sam has learning problems in school, but he is a good athlete and well liked by people of all ages. His mother and his stepfather have encouraged Sam to join sports teams, and they come to most of his games at school. His parents have also encouraged Sam's friendly nature by helping him get involved in a volunteer program with the elderly and in a neighborhood youth club.

To build children's self-esteem, parents need to recognize any attempts at cooperating with the family. Psychiatrist Alfred Adler created a term, *social interest*, that was described as the ability to give and take, or to cooperate to further the welfare of humankind.[4] Social interest occurs when interest in yourself and others is in harmony. Social interest is a major objective for new families as they learn ways to work together.

Focusing on any effort or contribution, not only on completed actions or outstanding behaviors, gives a wide span of possibilities for encouragement. There are many things that you could encourage in your family by focusing on an effort or a contribution. For example, has your child started to help you with simple tasks, such as emptying the wastebaskets or setting places at the table? The child might answer the phone and take a message for you that is incomplete, but at least you have the number or the name of the person who called. The idea is simple. Recognize and encourage any effort that moves in a positive direction.

Take the time to sit down and clearly identify the strengths, assets, resources, and potential of each of your children. What is it that you like about each of them? What are each child's most positive traits? Once you have identified these traits, focus intensely on them during this coming week. Immediately comment any time you observe these traits.

This will put you in a new position. You will be like an old-time gold prospector surveying the land. You may need to dig deep to find your "gold." You are looking at children who silently give the message "I have an asset or a resource. Can you find it?" When you do find the "gold," your relationship with your children will change.

Sometimes when parents are discouraged, they think there is nothing about a child that can be encouraged. They may quickly identify a child's negative traits, almost as if building a case for why the child can't be encouraged. It is possible, though, to think of the positive side of each of these traits. For example, if a teenager resists authority, could it mean that he is somebody who is willing to take a position or initiative? If a child is stubborn, could it mean that she is determined? Find ways to attach these apparently negative behaviors to a positive way of interacting with the child.

Ten-year-old Lin is unbending in her opinion. When she "knows she is right," her father, Kwong, cannot change her position. Kwong was always frustrated by this trait of Lin's until he was able to see it in a positive way. Instead of thinking of Lin as bullheaded, he began to think of Lin as not easily swayed or influenced by the crowd. Kwong decided this could be a very useful trait for Lin, particularly when dealing with peer pressure.

Seeing Alternatives

There are many ways of giving meaning to or viewing the same situation. For example, imagine your child comes home from school discouraged because he is bringing a paper on which he did poorly. To understand the source of your child's discouragement, you need to understand your child's view of the situation. Think of some alternatives. Your child could be discouraged because he feels he has disappointed you, disappointed himself, or disappointed his teacher. You even may think he is discouraged when he is not really concerned about grades, but you are.

"At least he's developing a good throwing arm!"

Every situation provides an opportunity to choose among alternative views and ways of reacting. If you can see alternative ways of viewing a situation or behavior (perceptual alternatives), you will be able to creatively look for the positive response. Even a school paper that has a low grade provides a positive opportunity to help a child explain his feelings and intentions. There are a variety of situations that might appear discouraging in your relationship with your child that you can turn into positive situations.

Using Humor

Humor helps people to see life and relationships in perspective. When people take a humorous approach they look at their rigid perceptions of themselves, their children, and their situations and see how this rigidity constricts all of their relationships. One way to see the humor in a situation is to ask yourself "What is the worst that could happen in this situation?" Exaggerating what could happen to the point of ridiculousness makes the situation seem less serious. The worst rarely happens, of course, and a sense of humor makes it easier to survive whatever does happen. Humor allows you to be more alive and more creative. It enables you to be in touch with all of your alternatives.

The Difference between Praise and Encouragment

Sometimes people tend to see encouragement as being the same as praise. There are some important differences, though, between the two concepts and their results. Encouragement is essential for producing change. Even though certain accomplishments may seem worthy of praise, encouraging accomplishments and attempts has more potential for better long-term results than praise. The differences between the basic characteristics and the possible results of praise and encouragement are summarized on the following chart.

Chart 2. Differences between Praise and Encouragement

Praise		Encouragement	
Basic Characteristics	*Possible Results*	*Basic Characteristics*	*Possible Results*
1. Focuses on external evaluations.	Children feel their value depends upon being acceptable to others. They feel self-esteem when they are doing what is acceptable, and they fear any negative comments.	Focuses on internal evaluations.	Children learn to assess their own status and to evaluate their progress. They rely upon their opinion, not the opinion of others as to their worth.
2. Focuses on reward for exceptional and completed task.	Children learn to set high standards and to measure their value by whether or not they are perfect. The fear of failure develops.	Recognizes any effort or improvement.	Children develop self-acceptance of their efforts. They develop the desire to try regardless of results.
3. Focuses on external control.	Children measure their worth by the ability to do what is expected. In some instances they learn to resist this type of force.	Focuses on children's ability to manage themselves positively.	Children develop the courage to be imperfect. This ability to be self-accepting provides growth. Self-confidence and responsibility for their own behavior is developed.

Note. Adapted with permission from American Guidance Service, Inc., Publishers' Bldg., Circle Pines, MN 55014. *Systematic Training for Effective Parenting: The Parent's Handbook* (p. 40) by Don Dinkmeyer and Gary D. McKay, Copyright 1982 (rev. ed.). Rights reserved.

Encouraging Words

Many parents would like to speak in a more positive, encouraging way to their children but don't know what to say. Sometimes their first efforts to make positive comments do not sound natural. For some parents focusing on the positive in contrast to focusing on mistakes is a new method of communication.

Remember your goals in the encouragement process. You are focusing on increasing your children's self-esteem, self-worth, and self-acceptance. You are not trying to communicate your opinion and make the children internalize your values. Instead, you want them to start to develop their own self-appraisal and sense of worth.

When encouraging your children, it is important to eliminate words that make only your values important. Don't say "That was great, excellent, superb, the best, outstanding!" Instead, learn to use words that express encouragement. These phrases are simple and still clearly enable you to communicate encouragement. Remember that encouragement demonstrates acceptance, focuses on contributions, recognizes any effort or attempt, and shows support. You could say something similar to the following.

> "You seem happy about that."
> "You look like you are enjoying that."
> "Tell me how you feel about that."
> "You're making it."
> "I appreciate your help."
> "I can see you put a lot of effort into that."
> "You seem pleased with your progress."
> "I see you've improved in _____."

The atmosphere for encouragement starts in the general family atmosphere. You can help create that atmosphere by refusing to be trapped into self-defeating behaviors and by not blaming others for failure. Probably the most important goals to keep in mind as you build your self-esteem and your children's self-esteem by the methods presented in this chapter are: have the courage to be imperfect and have confidence in your family structure. Take one day at a time and focus on small improvements, using them to encourage yourself and your family members. Your understanding of self-esteem and encouragement will be used in the next chapter as you look at the relationships in your family and your children's behavior goals.

Activity Assignment

During the next week, identify a strength of each one of your children and/or stepchildren and begin building on the identified strength. For example, if your child is good with tools you could ask the child's help in minor repairs around the house and show appreciation for the assistance.

Important Points to Remember in Chapter 2

1. Self-esteem is your inner confidence and feelings of self-worth that allow you to feel positive about yourself.

2. Encouragement is the process of focusing on an individual's resources in order to build that person's self-esteem and self-confidence.

3. People who encourage are able to see what is positive in any interaction.

4. Self-encouragement involves building a positive relationship with yourself, using self-valuing statements, and changing your discouraging beliefs.

5. Some common discouraging beliefs of single parents and stepfamily parents are:

-   "I must be in control and my children should not challenge me."
-   "The children should and must love me."
-   "I should be treated fairly."
-   "I know what's best."
-   "I must replace the absent parent."
-   "I must make it up to the children for their having only one parent at home."
-   "My divorce is a personal failure."
-   "My family must prove its worth to the community."

6. The courage to be imperfect allows you to take chances and make mistakes.

7. Encouragement improves relationships between parents and children, increases the cooperation in the family, and helps children develop confidence, self-reliance, and the ability to face challenges.

8. The skills of encouraging include:

-   Listening
-   Responding to feelings
-   Focusing on strengths, efforts, and contributions
-   Seeing alternatives
-   Using humor

9. Encouragement is different from praise because encouragement focuses on a child's internal evaluation, recognizes any effort or improvement, and builds children's ability to manage their own behavior positively.

10. Encouraging words show support without making a value judgment.

Chapter 3

Relationships and Behavior

New families require changed or new relationships. In single-parent families, the relationship between both the custodial and noncustodial parent and the children changes. In stepfamilies, the new relationships that are formed are more complex, with a stepparent and often stepsiblings being added to the family. This chapter explores the new relationships formed both in single-parent families and in stepfamilies. Later in the chapter you will also learn about the types of misbehavior that children may display when family relationships change.

New Relationships in the Single-Parent Family

A divorce takes place between spouses and not between parents and children. Sometimes self-esteem issues revolve around whether the ex-spouse and the ex-spouse's relatives should be included in the new single-parent family or stepfamily. A parent who is truly concerned about the children will not deny these loving contacts with the ex-spouse and the ex-spouse's relatives. These contacts can foster children's self-esteem because they give children an opportunity to feel valued and of worth. The stronger the parent's self-esteem, the more readily the parent will recognize the importance of the ex-spouse and the fact that this person can fit into the children's lives. Regardless of what a custodial parent feels for an ex-spouse, the parent needs to be supportive and positive about the noncustodial parent to the children. The ex-spouse needs to work out a relationship with the children in his own way. The goal of each parent is to relate positively with the children when the parent is with them.

The custodial parent's relationship with the children will usually grow stronger, particularly if there is only one child in the home. The parent and child may come to rely upon each other to keep the family going. Each person's contribution to the family becomes essential.

There are some changes in the relationship between single parents and children that can be expected. For example, an only child may have invested a great deal in the family. When loss occurs through divorce or death, the only child's security is threatened, and she may assume she needs to belong in a new way. The only child may turn to demonstrating helplessness or take on ambitious, adult-oriented, and protective qualities. Once she has passed a period of attempting to belong through helplessness, the child may move toward becoming a partner rather than a child. The single parent left to deal with the only child now has a new situation. According to Dr. Robert Brassington, who has researched the family constellation, "In all single parent family constellations there is a tendency on the

"Hi, Mom! I'll do the dishes for you after I fix the leak."

part of one or more of the children to step into the shoes of the absent parent, to assume that if they can fulfill this role the remaining parent will be satisfied and appreciative."[1]

In a two-child, single-parent family, typically the older child, who has been ambitious, cautious about taking risks, self-confident, and adult-oriented, may feel the need to continue to be first. In the single-parent family headed by a female where there is an older boy and a younger girl, there may be a reversal of roles in the children.

Divorced parents may find that they have a difficult time resolving their relationship with their ex-spouse. They may feel confused, guilty, angry, and anxious. If you feel that your relationship with your ex-spouse is unresolved, do not let your feelings influence your relationship with your children in any way. You will find a section on communicating with your ex-spouse in Chapter 8.

New Relationships in the Stepfamily

Stepfamilies require new relationships, and there will be some pain involved in developing these relationships. Many adjustments and compromises will need to be made if the new family is to function. Keeping in mind the differences between the nuclear family and the stepfamily and society's unrealistic expectations for all family members that you learned in Chapter 1 is a good place to start. The early stages before and after a remarriage are the appropriate places to begin building new relationships.

Courting and Remarriage
The courting process allows the couple time to get to know each other, resolve differences in child-rearing practices, and discuss emotional attachments to the ex-spouse. Legal divorce occurs in the courtroom, but emotional divorce occurs only when people begin to rebuild their own lives.

If the emotional business of the past is not dealt with during the courting process, the survival of the stepfamily may be in jeopardy. If people don't take time to resolve emotional leftovers from previous marriages, they tend to choose a new spouse with similar traits to the ex-spouse, and the same mistakes may occur in the second family as in the first.

> Mary was widowed three times before the age of 40. All three husbands were depressive and suicidal. Each death was followed almost immediately by remarriage.
>
> The first husband deliberately drove his car off a bridge into a deep ravine. Husband number two was diabetic and refused to follow medical advice. He abused his health by excessive drinking, overeating, and neglecting to take insulin until he went into a coma and could not be revived. Mary's third husband accidentally shot himself while in an alcoholic stupor. All three men shared similar personality characteristics and used depression to punish and control others.

If Mary had taken the time to examine why she chose her first husband, she might have ended this serial marriage cycle after husband number one. Taking the time to learn about yourself and the traits of a potential spouse is well worth the investment and will help prevent problems that could result in the failure of a second family. If you have difficulty doing this, you may want to seek professional assistance.

Once a relationship is proceeding to marriage, it is helpful for both sets of children to feel they are part of the process. There is a greater chance of winning the children's cooperation if they have time to get to know the potential stepparent and stepsiblings.

Include the children in planning family outings. These should be planned in advance with everyone's needs being considered. A planning meeting will acquaint children with two concepts: the model for a family meeting and how to negotiate so each person feels her opinion was considered. This process will provide practice for resolving more difficult issues the members may face when they become a family. Chapter 6 provides detailed information on family meetings and negotiation.

To help the new family get a good start, it is better if both families leave their previous homes and select a new house or apartment, if possible. This enables the new family to begin building their own traditions in a new setting. The children need to have some part in the selection of a new home and the choice of bedrooms.[2]

Another option might be to leave one house or apartment and move into the other one. However, this would require a lot of open discussion to deal with possible feelings of resentment. The new stepparent and the stepparent's children might feel like intruders in someone else's house if the previous spouse's imprint is still there in terms of wallpaper, paint, pictures, furniture arrangement, and what goes where in the kitchen cabinets. The new family needs no ghosts from the past to hinder them in making a fresh start. Therefore, if this option must be selected, the family should rearrange furniture and storage areas, using everyone's ideas and possessions. New paint and wallpaper can also help.

One additional recommendation is to compromise on the location of a new home (if possible) so the children can remain in the same school district, retain old friends, and take part in neighborhood activities. Children feel more secure when everything doesn't change at once. This will demonstrate that both stepfamily parents care about the children's feelings.

Dr. Paul Druckman, a family therapist in Toronto, believes that there are three areas stepfamilies need to consider when they are forming a new family.[3] These are also important for single-parent families to consider.

1. *Doing basic jobs and chores.* These include the jobs of preparing meals, caring for clothing, cleaning the house, maintaining the yard, and so on.

2. *Providing opportunities for people in the family to develop both emotionally and intellectually.* This involves developing communication in which people actually hear what others say and negotiate compromises. This, of course, is different from the instant obedience that is sometimes anticipated by parents.

3. *Preparing family members to cope with the world as it actually is outside of the family.* This suggests that instead of demanding obedience and imposing controls, parents need to teach their children to negotiate their way through life.

When the new family structure is created, look for all of the assets and resources that have been gathered in the new setting. After the family has become acquainted with each other and lived together for a while, a good exercise is to have each person share first what they like about themselves and then what they like about various members of the family. Then, as the family continues to form, it will be helpful to encourage and find the positive in any cooperative effort of family members.

The Couple's Relationship
Keeping a marriage enthusiastic, loving, and involved is a challenging task. A couple in a stepfamily may face conflicts, unrealistic expectations, and attempts by the children to break the couple's bond. The children need to understand and accept the central importance of the couple's relationship. The parents are not trying to seek the children's approval of their relationship.

The couple's relationship forms a base for the family.

The fact is that the couple's relationship is the primary one in the family. When a couple's relationship is weak, the entire family relationship is weakened.

Stepfamily parents must take time for their relationship as a couple. Unless they have developed a high level of satisfaction in their marriage, they will not find it possible to develop a happy, successful stepfamily.

It may help parents to become involved in a marriage enrichment program, which develops skills of dialogue, encouragement, and conflict resolution.[4] Stepfamily parents need to find a balance between the amount of time they spend with each other as a couple, the amount of time that they spend with their own children and with the stepchildren, and the amount of time that they spend on their individual interests and needs. All of these times are basic to developing individual and family self-esteem and cooperation.

It is important for couples to support each other as parents. While it may seem obvious, often it is not. When the new family begins, born out of the remarriage, parenting styles often will be incompatible. One parent may be autocratic, demanding, and relentless in pursuit of control and establishment of boundaries. The other parent may be permissive, accepting, and a pushover for any misbehavior that occurs. Parents need to develop compatible parenting styles, while respecting differences in styles. Chapter 7 discusses how parents can negotiate their different parenting styles.

Stepparents and Children
Stepparents often have a real desire to be parents and have something specific in mind about raising a son or daughter. They may see stepparenting as a special opportunity and be determined to establish a special relationship with their stepchildren. They may put a lot of effort and energy into the relationship and set some very specific goals for both the relationship and the children.

Stepparents can become disillusioned when they don't get the love, obedience, and cooperation they had hoped for from the children. They frequently believe that they have made a major investment and there should be some payoff. Unfortunately, no matter how determined the stepparent is, it's difficult to be totally accepted by the stepchildren. Stepparents are trying to find a place for themselves in a group that is already established.

Stepparents are also often discouraged when they find they have no legal status with regard to their stepchildren. Special provisions must be made to include them in a family inheritance. Stepchildren, too, are often dismayed to find when they are adults that the person they accepted as a parent is not legally their parent.

Children usually see stepparents as intruders and may resent them—particularly if the stepparent's children are to become part of the new family unit. Many children resent any attempted replacement of a parent through remarriage. They may misbehave or refuse to cooperate, putting stress on the new parental and spousal relationships. For example, a usually cooperative child may suddenly refuse or forget to do a previously agreed upon chore. Or a child may show open resentment of the new stepparent through direct disobedience or angry shouting matches.

This misbehavior can be ignored for the moment and dealt with at a family meeting, using listening skills and problem solving. (The family meeting is discussed in Chapter 6.) The child can learn that while the stepparent is not attempting to interfere with the child's relationship with the biological parent, the stepparent does have a right to expect to be part of the family. Helping children learn to cope with resentment develops their ability to deal with the stresses that occur in the changing family structure.

Many stepparents are so concerned about being accepted that they create problems by pushing too hard. The more they push, the more conflict they are likely to encounter. The biological parent may feel guilty because the children are not cooperating. Children sense the stepfamily parents' concerns and may attempt to manipulate both parents. This may result in a battle with parents on one side and children on the other. At this point many parents realize they are outnumbered and attempt to win the children's approval by trying to please them or becoming slaves. The outcome of this may be a houseful of tyrants. When parents get tired of this situation and decide to exert their authority, the conflict escalates.

The family meeting provides opportunities to discuss these issues and teach the children how to negotiate. New relationships require open, honest, sensitive communication of feelings by both adults and children. Regular family meetings also help the stepfamily learn to get along with each other and strengthen the feeling of belonging to the new family unit.

In an attempt to impress their new spouse and win the children over, many stepparents make the mistake of competing with their new partner's ex-spouse. They hold the unrealistic expectation that they can replace the biological parent by "outparenting" them. One example of this might be the stepfather who believes he can buy the children's love by giving them treats their father cannot supply. Another example could be the stepmother who turns her kitchen into a gourmet restaurant for picky eaters to outdo the children's mother.

These tactics are doomed to failure because children aren't stupid. They will understand the "game" and either use it to their advantage, resent it, or do both. The outcome may be increasing competition between the noncustodial parent and the stepparent resulting in angry confrontations. Nobody really wins in this kind of situation, but the stepparent almost always becomes the big loser— the stepparent's relationship with the children suffers.

It is important for stepparents to respect the children's existing roles in the family. The first-time parent, in particular, often tries to be too controlling and as a result meets a lot of resistance. If the responsibilities the children had in the single-parent family increased their self-esteem, then those roles should continue even though the new spouse may want to move in and take over such responsibilities. Children from a single-parent family in which they have had to take care of themselves typically lose some self-esteem when the stepfamily is formed. They are now required to be responsible and cooperate with a new parental figure who is going to "make things better for everybody." If the children have been contributing, they should be reinforced and encouraged.

A stepparent who enters a family that includes a teenager needs to realize that teenagers are emerging adults who are in the process of separating from the family in order to establish an adult identity. The stepparent may experience resistance if she attempts to take over some of the teenager's responsibilities and restrict the teenager's freedom. There is a greater chance of winning the teenager's cooperation if he is encouraged to continue with his usual responsibilities and freedoms. The teenager needs to know his contributions are appreciated and that he is important to the family.

The task of the stepparent is to be a positive role model in the family. A positive way to approach the stepparent role is to develop a unique relationship with the children. This relationship does not seek to replace the one each child has with the absent biological parent. It will be a new and different relationship—like the relationship established when making a new friend. Stepparents should keep in mind that their roles with the children may vary based on each child's age. For example, a young child may want nurturing from the stepparent while an older child may see attempts to nurture as usurping the biological parent's role.

Relationships based on their own special characteristics have a better chance of succeeding than those in which stepparents try to replace the biological parent. Since relationships are built on common interests, stepparents need to work at finding something to share with the children. This might be a hobby or an interest unique to the stepparent and the child.

If you are a stepparent, remember to be patient and don't push. It takes time to build a new relationship. As the children have a chance to show love, the resentment, jealousy, and guilt they may be experiencing will be reduced. They will develop a relationship with you on their terms and in their time.

Ned had been able to establish a relationship with all of his stepchildren except Marvella. Ten-year-old Marvella constantly spoke about the fun she used to have playing softball and basketball with her father. She got angry at Ned, who was not very athletic, when he tried to play with her. One day after some stinging criticism from Marvella, Ned went into the family room to cool down by playing video games. Marvella came into the room later and they discovered that they both loved video games. Playing video games together became a nonthreatening way to have fun together and to build a base of shared experiences.

Stepsiblings

One of the most important things that may happen in a remarriage is a shift in the positions the children have developed in the family. For example, the new family may have two firstborns competing for the role they played in the nuclear family. Stepfamily parents can help both children see they are of equal value. It is possible to win their cooperation and reduce competition by explaining that help from both of them is needed because of the increased number of children and chores. Their leadership skills can be encouraged, and they can be asked to help solve problems by working together to come up with ideas and solutions. The important point is that they work together to come up with mutually agreeable solutions.

These transitions in families are often very challenging. They are positive in the sense that children learn to be flexible in new roles, but may distress children as their position changes. Each child is in the process of finding a way to become significant in the family and in the world. Parents need to support each child in becoming a person with self-esteem, social interest, and a sense of humor.

Most adults assume that stepsiblings are just like siblings in a nuclear family, but actually stepsiblings bear no more relationship to each other than acquaintances. The sexual taboos that apply to sisters and brothers in nuclear families do not automatically work in stepfamilies. Therefore, if nonrelated teenagers inhabiting the same house become more than friends, there is a chance the relationship could become sexual. A frank discussion about what is acceptable in the new family will usually suffice. If it does not, other living arrangements may have to be made for one of the teenagers.

Time with Children

The amount of time parents spend with their children will change when the single-parent family or stepfamily forms. A single parent, possibly becoming both the breadwinner and the homemaker, may find it challenging to put time into effective parenting. Stepparents may find time they used to spend with their own children is now shared with the new spouse and stepchildren. The amount of time you spend with your children is not as important, however, as the way in which the time is spent. You can discuss with your family the options available for time spent together. These guidelines will help you make the most of the time you spend with a child.

1. Be totally present. Do not be distracted by other people or situations. If you get a phone call, tell the caller you will return the call later.
2. Listen closely to what is being communicated.
3. Participate in activities involving the child's goals and interests. However, times that are going to be mutually enjoyable are best. Find activities that both you and your child enjoy.
4. Be encouraging and accepting.

Misbehavior and the New Family Structure

When a marriage deteriorates or a new family forms, children's misbehavior and lack of cooperation may increase. Children recognize the vacuum in power caused when a parent leaves and the imbalance created when a stepparent and stepsiblings are added to the family. The children may try to find their place in the family in a new and unique way. They may have been well settled into the previous family structure, cooperative, helpful, and seldom presenting a problem. When the family changes, they may revert to old misbehaviors or try out some new ones. For example, a child may attempt to get special attention from one parent because the other biological parent is no longer available. The child may attempt to assert power to obtain a new position in the family or feel hurt and strive to get even.

It is important to accept this misbehavior as typical and not give in or feel sorry for the child's mistaken perceptions and faulty behavior. Children need to be respected, enjoyed, and encouraged during the formation of a new family. At the same time, however, it is equally important that you be both firm and kind in establishing limits on misbehavior.

The Goals of Misbehavior

All behavior has a purpose. Often people tend to think of behavior as being without explanation or as having been caused by some external event. While heredity and environment do influence behavior, behavior is usually directed by a goal. That goal is the way in which a child seeks to belong and become part of a group. Understanding the purpose of behavior is important because it enables you to have an optimistic way of looking at your children's development and behavior. Your children are decision-making, social beings, whose main goal is to belong. They strive continually to find and maintain for themselves a place of significance.

Misbehaving children are discouraged. They do not think they can belong in active, constructive ways. Instead, they feel they will be recognized because of their misbehavior. Rudolf Dreikurs, a prominent psychiatrist, classified misbehavior into four categories or goals:[5]

- Attention
- Power
- Revenge
- Display of inadequacy

These are negative goals because they cannot help an individual grow or develop. They interfere with children's development of positive goals. The purpose of a child's misbehavior can be understood by observing the consequences of the behavior.

1. Observe your own reactions to the child's misbehavior. Your feelings help you identify the child's goal.

2. Observe the child's response to your attempts at correction. How the child responds to your behavior will also confirm the goal.[6]

Through these observations, you will gain a new perspective on misbehavior. You will no longer be trying to understand what caused the behavior but will become aware of the purpose of the behavior.

Attention

Most children, especially young children, want attention. They can get attention through positive, constructive behavior or negative behavior. The attention-seeking child approaches the parent in a way that is difficult to ignore. When there has been a change in the family situation, all of the children may seek special attention for a time. The parents may feel the children's behavior has regressed and former behaviors may reappear.

If your child develops a feeling that she belongs only when she is noticed or receiving special attention, you will need to

"Dad! Dad! Look at me!"

ignore most negative bids for attention. You can do this more systematically if you are aware of your feelings. If you are annoyed by your child's behavior and tend to correct the behavior with a reminder, then the child has received what she is looking for—attention. The bid for attention is confirmed if the child stops the misbehavior at that time and misbehaves later or finds another way to get attention. She may stop making noise and a bit later start again or fight with a sibling.

Some children get attention by acting as if they can only function if their parents work with them or help them. The parents can become enslaved because the children "need" the attention.

Power
Power-seeking children feel recognized or think they belong when they feel in control. They seek to do only what they want and are determined not to be forced to do anything against their will. Children who seek power may do so actively or passively. For example, children who are stubborn and defeat their parents through inactivity are seeking power passively.

Parents usually try to prove to power-seeking children that they cannot win or boss the parents around. When such children are controlled, however, they seem to become more aggressive and develop an even greater interest in power. They may for a time defiantly give in to their parents. The parents may win the power struggle, but lose the relationship. Furthermore, the parents teach the children exactly the opposite of what they probably want to teach them; they teach that whoever has the most power wins.

When your child seeks power, you may feel you are always challenged and be angry. Any attempt to correct the child is usually defeated, and the unacceptable behavior continues.

Revenge
Children who seek revenge are convinced that they are not loveable. They feel significant only when they are able to get even, as they feel they have been treated cruelly or unfairly. Revengeful children earn a place by being cruel and disliked.

They know how to strike at exactly the point that hurts most. They may also seek revenge through passive means.

When your child seeks revenge, you feel discouraged and very hurt and want to get even. If you attack the child, the child will become even more intensely vengeful.

Display of Inadequacy

Children who display inadequacy are the most discouraged of all. They appear to have given up any hope of being successful. Instead, they try to keep others from expecting them to function. They have low self-esteem, caused by their belief that they are only adequate if they perform well. They usually give up in areas such as schoolwork, athletics, or music where they believe they can't meet their parents' standards. You know if your child is displaying inadequacy because you feel despair, hopelessness, and want to give up. The child usually responds in a passive way to your first attempts to change her behavior, and you eventually quit trying.

Helping Children Develop Positive Behavior Goals

Once you understand the goal of a child's behavior, you can redirect the child into more active, positive, and constructive behavior. Children's behavior, however, changes only as the parents change their approach. Parents are not necessarily the cause of children's misbehavior, but they often unintentionally reinforce and encourage the goals of the misbehavior. Your most important first step in changing your child's misbehavior is to change yourself and your typical responses to the misbehavior. Obviously, the responses that you have been giving tend to reinforce the behavior.

The following are general guidelines for helping your children develop positive behavior goals. You will learn specific procedures based on these guidelines in Chapter 7.

Helping Children Who Seek Attention

Develop opportunities for children who seek attention to be involved, to cooperate, and to be a part of the family. By appreciating and recognizing this cooperation, you will encourage more socially acceptable behavior and less attention getting.

If your child often selects passive or destructive ways to get attention, you need to change your responses to help the child achieve recognition through positive, useful contributions rather than through negative, useless bids for attention. Focus on any constructive behavior while ignoring misbehavior. Certain misbehaviors require attention, *but* the attention is given in a way that is not anticipated.

Learn to avoid giving attention for negative behavior and instead attend to positive behavior; give your attention not when it demanded but when it is unexpected. Do not communicate that the child only belongs when being noticed or served. You do not want to reinforce the child's belief that "I am special and must be treated specially."

> Five-year-old Karl banged a spoon on the bottom of a saucepan whenever his mother, Helga, watched the nightly news on televi-

sion. When she corrected him, Karl would stop for a few minutes and then begin another noisy game, such as slamming cupboard doors open and shut. Helga decided to ignore the noise and attend to Karl's positive behavior some time after the news was over. She found this worked better in changing Karl's behavior than continually correcting him.

Helping Children Who Seek Power

Give children who seek power the chance to make their own decisions and to be responsible for their own behavior. This will allow them to become more autonomous and independent. As they make their own decisions, encourage them to accept the consequences of their behavior and express confidence in their judgment. Encourage children as they become more mature and feel less need to get their way.

When you deal with a power-seeking child you need to refrain from showing your negative feelings, particularly your anger. You need to get away from the power struggle. If you use power in retaliation, your child will only be impressed with the value of power and more motivated to use power.

> Nina and her stepmother, Annie, always argued about where the dishes and canned goods should be stored in the kitchen. When Annie moved things to cupboards she found convenient, Nina always moved them back to the places in which they had been before Annie had joined the family. Often things were out of reach of Annie, who was very short. After a few weeks of this, Annie stopped arguing and asked Nina to help her pick out new places for everything in the kitchen, most of which would be convenient for both of them, and to shop with her for a kitchen ladder that Annie could use.

Helping Children Who Seek Revenge

Teach revengeful children how to be more cooperative and equal by showing them love and respect. These children in particular need to be shown lots of respect, and it is important that they are treated equally. They often seek their rights. By showing respect for a revengeful child and her rights, you give the child a model for leading a life of mutual respect.

The most important thing to do is to avoid the tendency to feel hurt and retaliate. Even though you may have strong feelings of hurt, you can't improve a relationship through retaliation. Revengeful behavior is a symptom of discouragement and not necessarily a result of past parental behavior. You need to find a way to develop some point of positive contact and cooperation. There is always something positive that you can comment on, support, and encourage.

> Melanie planted 2 dozen petunias in the yard and her 12-year-old stepdaughter, Tanith, cut them down while mowing the grass. Tanith claimed she hadn't noticed them, but Melanie felt very hurt because Tanith often "accidentally" destroyed Melanie's possessions. Melanie usually punished Tanith for such behavior but decided to ignore it this time. Instead, she concentrated on showing respect for Tanith and commenting on her positive behavior.

Helping Children Who Display Inadequacy

Encouragement is most important in helping children who display inadequacy. All criticism should be eliminated. The focus instead will be on the child's assets and strengths. Any effort or attempt, no matter how insignificant it may seem, should be recognized.

You can also help the child to use withdrawal positively. Withdrawal, if not used to avoid being assertive, is useful for refusing to initiate arguments and avoiding conflicts.

> Ten-year-old Tom seemed hopeless to his father, Henry. Tom was failing academically and was too uncoordinated to play sports. Tom couldn't even dry dishes without breaking a plate or glass. Henry felt unable to help his son and instead constantly criticized him. One day after Tom broke an entire set of mugs, Henry caught himself before he became critical. He helped Tom clean up without saying a word and later that day encouraged Tom in the one area in which he seemed competent—working with animals.

Remember that your children's negative behavior goals can be changed. The following chart will summarize for you how to deal with your children's goals of misbehavior.

Chart 3. Dealing with the Goals of Misbehavior

Child's Belief	Goal	Parent's Feelings	Child's Response to Parent's Attempts to Correct	Major Alternatives for Parents
I belong when I am noticed or receiving special attention.	Attention	Annoyed	Temporarily stops misbehavior and then repeats or finds another way to get attention.	Develop opportunities for cooperation. Ignore misbehavior when possible. Attend to positive behavior when not expected.
I belong when I am in control and prove no one can boss me.	Power	Angry, challenged	Increases aggressive behavior or gives in defiantly.	Help child to make decisions and be responsible for behavior. Remove self from conflict.
I belong by hurting and getting even.	Revenge	Discouraged, deeply hurt, and wants to get even	Intensifies revengeful behavior.	Show respect. Avoid punishing and retaliating. Build a trusting relationship.
I belong by convincing others to expect nothing from me.	Display of inadequacy	Hopelessness, despair	Is passive, makes no response. Parent gives up attempting to correct.	Eliminate criticism. Encourage any effort. Focus on assets.

Note. Adapted with permission from American Guidance System, Inc., Publishers' Bldg., Circle Pines, MN 55014. *Systematic Training for Effective Parenting: The Parent's Handbook* (p. 14) by Don Dinkmeyer and Gary D. McKay, Copyright 1982 (rev. ed.). Rights reserved.

The positive behavior goal is one that helps the individual develop self-respect and respect for others. Children with positive behavior goals are motivated by a relationship of mutual respect. As you help your children develop positive goals, focus on any positive behavior, however slight. Your ability to encourage any attempt or effort, your sense of humor, and your ability to see things in perspective will help your children develop positive goals and will help build the relationships in your family. Your own and your children's personality and emotions play a large part in your children's behavior goals and the relationships in your family, as presented in the next chapter.

Activity Assignment

During the next week, plan and carry out ways to spend quality time with each of your children and/or stepchildren.

Important Points to Remember in Chapter 3

1. Custodial and noncustodial parents each work out the relationship with the children in their own way. Children usually become very close to the parent in a single-parent family.

2. Children in a single-parent family may demonstrate helplessness or take on adult qualities and attempt to fill the role of the other parent.

3. The process of building relationships in a stepfamily can begin during the couple's courting phase.

4. Three areas that stepfamilies need to consider when they form the new family are:

- Doing basic jobs and chores
- Providing opportunities for people in the family to develop both emotionally and intellectually
- Preparing family members to cope with the world as it actually is outside of the family

5. Stepfamily parents must take time for the couple relationship and balance the time they spend together, alone, and with the children.

6. Stepparents cannot expect instant love from their stepchildren and must build relationships with them similar to those with friends.

7. Stepsiblings are not like brothers and sisters in a nuclear family. They may compete for their birth order positions in the stepfamily or become sexually attracted to each other.

8. The amount of time you spend with children is not as important to the children's development as the way your time with them is spent.

9. When the family structure changes, children may try to find their place in the family through misbehavior.

10. The four goals of misbehavior are:

- Attention
- Power
- Revenge
- Display of inadequacy

11. You can recognize your child's goal of misbehavior by your feelings and your child's reaction to correction.

- Parents feel annoyed with children who seek attention. When corrected, the children stop their misbehavior and misbehave again later.
- Parents feel challenged and angry with children who seek power. When corrected, the children become more aggressive or defiantly give in.
- Parents feel discouraged, hurt, and vengeful with children who seek revenge. When corrected, the children become more revengeful.
- Parents feel despair and hopelessness with children who display inadequacy. If corrected, the children are passive.

12. The most important step in changing your child's misbehavior is to change yourself and your typical response to the behavior.

13. You can help children develop positive behavior goals by:

- Giving children who seek attention a chance to be involved and cooperate
- Letting children who seek power make their own decisions and be responsible for their own behavior
- Teaching revengeful children how to be more cooperative and equal by showing them love and respect
- Encouraging children who display inadequacy and eliminating all criticism

Chapter 4

Personality and Emotional Development

Each person has a unique personality that results from the way he perceives, understands, and organizes the world. Beliefs, goals, emotions, perceptions, and attitudes make up the personality and influence the way in which each person behaves. Similarly, each person has a unique lifestyle that is formed early in life as a result of his interpretation of his life experiences. Lifestyle can be thought of as the unifying aspect of personality. It includes beliefs about self, others, and one's place in the world. Because these beliefs were formed in early childhood, they are often not recognized by individuals.

People are not just passive receivers of their personality and lifestyle, but play an active, creative part in forming them. In this chapter, you will learn how personality develops, the goals that guide personality and behavior, and how people create their emotions, behavior, and lifestyle.

Heredity

It is not possible to determine the exact influence of heredity on personality and lifestyle. It is clear that heredity does have some influence. For example, a child who is short and uncoordinated may develop personality traits to compensate for his physical limitations. Unable to attract attention through physical prowess, he may become a clown or act as if he is incompetent and others must serve him. This child may develop a lifestyle designed to emphasize these traits.

There is, of course, little you can do about your children's hereditary characteristics. The one thing you can do is to help with what your children *believe* about these characteristics. Do this through focusing on assets, strengths, and resources, while minimizing liabilities.

The Family Atmosphere and Values

The family atmosphere results from the relationships between the parents and the children. The atmosphere may be, for example, overprotective, overindulgent, rejecting, authoritarian, permissive, or competitive. These discouraging family atmospheres have the potential to lower children's self-esteem and self-confidence and promote irresponsibility and discouragement about their ability to meet the challenges of life.

Family atmospheres that are more encouraging may focus primarily on developing independence, respect, acceptance, equality, realistic standards, confidence, consistent discipline, encouragement, the expression of feelings, and cooperation. In a family with an encouraging atmosphere, children are likely to become more self-reliant and responsible, experience self-worth and feel self-esteem, and set realistic goals.

The family values have a significant effect on the development of personality and lifestyle. Family values are anything important to either parent, regardless of whether the parents agree or disagree about the value. The values may concern, for example, education, the use of money, athletics, the definition of success, religion, obedience, and hard work. The family values essentially give the child a message about what is important. They therefore place certain demands on the child.

Family values are significant in development because each child takes a stand in regard to the family values. The child may conform, rebel, or side with one parent against the other. The child will not remain neutral on a family value.

Children who conform accept the family values and go in the direction intended by the parent, even though they may demonstrate constructive or destructive behaviors. On the other hand, rebellious children resist family values and recognize that they can decide about the values for themselves. Sometimes the decision produces positive behavior. In other instances it results in

Sometimes a child's choices about family values
may take him down a different path.

negative behavior. Many children accept certain family values
and reject others.

When the family structure changes, the family values may be
challenged. For example, does the single parent still hold to
some of the values that appeared to be important to the family
when two parents were present? What is the role of the noncustodial parent in influencing values?

Sunday dinners at Brad's mother's house were always a formal
affair. Everyone wore his best clothes, and the table was set with
the best china and crystal. At his father's new home, everyone
made sandwiches for dinner and no one ate together. Brad spent
every other weekend with his father and did not like the informal
Sunday dinners very much. Although he didn't complain when he
was with his father, he decided that when he had his own family,
he would carry on his mother's tradition of making Sunday
dinner a special occasion.

The stepfamily brings together people with varying family values. As these people form a new family, there will be an opportunity to sort out values. Values that previously had been rejected by each family can be reconsidered. It is important not to attempt to remove or challenge values that children have already internalized, unless they are antisocial. Each child needs to be accepted as a person with no demands for change.

Parents play an important role by being available to explore values with their children. It is not the parents' role to impose values on the children. Instead, through open and honest communication, children can learn more about themselves and the things they want to pursue. For a value to have a real influence in a person's life, it needs to have been explored and experienced.

When a value is important to you, share your value clearly with your children, but avoid imposing the value. Do not attack the values of your children because at the same time you will be attacking the children personally. You can influence your children most through your own example and through listening and discussing.

You are a role model for your children. They learn more from what you do than what you say. They observe your behavior, your attitude, and what seems to work for you. They then select for themselves the qualities they value and want. Remember that your behavior will communicate more than your words. At times you'll be disappointed when it appears that your children tend to pick up more of your negative than positive traits. This may be because those appear to be the traits that work most effectively for you. For example, you may notice your child insists on getting his way. You find this upsetting. However, you are aware that many times you function in a demanding way and refuse to take no for an answer. If you stop being demanding, your behavior will influence your child to change.

The Family Constellation

Parents are generally thought of as the primary influence on the personality development of their children. However, it is now apparent that the personal meaning children develop from their position in the family is a very significant factor in the development of personality.

The *family constellation* is the psychological position of each child in relation to his sisters and brothers. Each child is born into a unique set of circumstances. The firstborn is an only child until a second child arrives and the firstborn is dethroned. The second child, and all ensuing children, deal with a sibling who is always ahead of them, except in special situations.

Siblings feel a need to compete for their position in the family. If one child is doing very well in school, the other child may attempt to do well in school also. If that attempt is not successful, the child may give up and become first in some other trait or skill. Or, a younger sibling may decide the older one is so successful that there is no sense in trying to compete. This sibling then chooses another area in which to make a mark, perhaps a negative area.

Only children have a unique position in the family; they don't have any siblings to compete with, so they are often the center of attention and they love it! They may feel privileged, special, and entitled to get what they want and have their own way. But they may also feel incompetent since they live in a world of adults and feel inadequate when they compare themselves to adults. They may compete with one parent for the affection of the other and often play divide and conquer. Only children often become very creative because they have to learn how to operate in a world of adults and often spend time alone, which brings opportunities for invention. Since they are both the oldest and the youngest child, they often have the strivings of the eldest and the feelings of inadequacy and demands of the youngest. Only children may have peer problems when they are children but better relations when they become adults—they are now official members of the world they know.

Oldest children are often interested in being first, pleasing, and controlling. They are usually successful in these endeavors until the second child is born, when they may feel unloved, neglected, and rejected. They may work to recapture their parents' attention through being especially good, responsible, and competent. Or they may choose to be the "best at being the worst" and excel through misbehavior.

Second children have to share their parents' attention. They may deal with their position of being second by becoming "hyper" and "pushy" and "running hard" to overtake their older sibling. They often choose the opposite role from the oldest. For example, they may develop the social skills with peers the first child may lack. Some second children choose the position of the rebel if their older sibling is successful. If a third child is born, the second child becomes a middle child.

Middle children find themselves sandwiched between an oldest who has all the rights and a youngest who has all the advantages. Where does that leave them? Some feel they don't really have a place in the family and see themselves as neglected, rejected, and unfortunate. They may become the family's "problem child." Others take the attitude "I can handle my brothers and sisters" and become the shining star, pushing the others down to elevate themselves. Regardless of which role they choose, the strength of middle children lies in their adaptability as they learn to relate to both their older and younger siblings.

Middle children of large families are often less competitive than middle children of three. Parents of large families don't have much time for each individual child; therefore the children usually learn to cooperate with each other in order to get what they want.

Youngest children often behave like only children. They see everyone as bigger and more competent. They often demand and get lots of service from family members who can't wait to fulfill their every wish, make their decisions, and handle their responsibilities. Consequently, they may feel very inadequate and weak, yet they are quite powerful in demanding and getting service. They can choose to be charming or quite negative in their pursuit of being served. Some youngest children decide they can overtake everyone, leave the baby role, charge up their engines, and speed past everyone on their way to the top!

Although this section presented only five positions—only, oldest, second, middle, and youngest—other positions such as third or fourth can be represented by one or more of the five

Each child seeks a place in the family in his own way.

basic positions. A child born third in a family of four, for example, could be psychologically the youngest of three, oldest of two, or an only child if there are large age differences between surrounding siblings. This child could also be in a dual position, taking on characteristics of two positions, such as the youngest of three and oldest of two.

While children's roles are often related to birth order, this is not always the case. The choice of a role is based on the children's perceptions of what it takes to belong in the family and how they can achieve a place. The sex of the child may make a difference if the family values one sex over the other. Children of the unfavored sex may feel special and may try to perform like the favored sex or may rebel against the preferred sex role. Cultural differences, changes in family structure, and age differences in siblings may also affect the family constellation. Since lifestyle is formed for most people between the ages of 4 and 6, a difference in age between siblings of 5 years can change the constellation. For example, an oldest child who is 5 years older than the next child may act more like an only child.

The family atmosphere and values account for many similarities among siblings while the family constellation and the competition between siblings account for many of the differences. A child's personality is most influenced by the sibling with whom he has the greatest degree of competition. This is usually the sibling closest in age to the child.

A person's behavior and feelings of satisfaction, worth, and value come from a desire to achieve and feel acceptance and belonging. When the form of the family changes, a child's view of how to maintain a place and how to be recognized, significant, and accepted is frequently altered.

Personality Priorities

A person's orientation to life has a consistent influence upon his relationships. However, some generalizations about life, developed when a person was young, may not always be true.

If you believe that you must be first, have to compete, or that it is horrible if others don't accept you, you will shape your relationships to be consistent with these beliefs. The basic beliefs and perceptions that you hold can strengthen or injure your relationships. You need to be aware of your beliefs and how they influence your relationships, particularly the relationship with your children.

Priorities, people's decisions about what is important in their lives, are reflected in their ways of relating to others. People develop a sense of belonging by pursuing their priorities. When you determine what you value in your relationships, you become aware of your priorities. Four common personality priorities are:

- To be superior
- To be in control
- To please others
- To maintain your own comfort[1]

When we are self-accepting, possess self-esteem and a sense of humor, and no longer believe we have to be special to belong, then we have the healthiest priority—social interest, or to cooperate with others to further society's interest.[2] It is the willingness to participate in the give and take of life.

Your personality priorities can influence the way in which you relate to your children and the way in which you parent. For example, if you place a greater value on pleasing and superiority than on comfort and control, you may feel defeat when you are not pleasing your children or being superior.

It is important to understand that no one priority can summarize a person or is better than the other priorities. All of the priorities have their strengths and limitations. Most people probably act on a combination of priorities. The beliefs that undergird the personality priorities may be expressed in either positive or negative ways.

Being Superior

People who value superiority may believe they need to be better than others. Unless they are the best, life has little meaning. It is important to them to prove that they are more competent, more right, and more useful than others. A person who values superiority may believe:

1. "I must be the best."
2. "I have to be perfect."
3. "I am special and should be treated as special."

People who value superiority often feel overburdened and uncertain and may fear failure and defeat. Their relationships may be in doubt. They may complain of too much to do in too little time and guilt feelings. The child of a person whose priority is superiority may feel, "I can't do anything right," "I'm never good enough," "I just can't live up to my parent's standards," or "I have to be superior and perfect."

> Toby had been the valedictorian of his senior class, as well as the class president and captain of the track team. He continued to value being the best and pushed himself to high achievements in college and in his career. He became irritated when his son Mackie seemed to be content to get average grades in high school and was more interested in having fun than "making something special of himself."

People with superiority as a priority have a number of positive qualities. These people can be creative and use their assets to help their children develop. They can decide, for example, to be more accepting of their own and their children's mistakes—modeling the courage to be imperfect. Since they often have a positive outlook on life, they can encourage their children to be contributors.

Controlling

People who place a high value on control may control others through intelligence, temper, charm, stubbornness, being dependent, or being resistant. They may operate on the fear that unless they control others, they will be humiliated. Controllers want to avoid embarrassment at all costs. They may complain of lacking friends and not feeling close to others. They are cautious about the unexpected and fear ridicule. Beliefs of controllers include:

1. "I must be in control of myself and others."
2. "I must have my own way."
3. "I must be the boss."

If a person places a high value on self-control, she may have difficulty acknowledging her feelings. Her children may believe it's not safe to share their feelings with her. Because people generally don't want to be controlled by others, they tend to choose not to get close to someone who is controlling. Controllers stay distant so others can't control them. Thus, controllers frequently feel they are not a part of things.

> Jacob values being in control and feels it is important to be in charge of everything. He tends to overcontrol so that things are run "smoothly." He tells his stepchildren what to wear in the morning, supervises chores that they can do without his help, and tries to organize all of their leisure time. When something comes up that Jacob can't control, such as unexpected delays and changes in a family outing, he becomes very uncomfortable and anxious.

However, people who value control may be well organized and tend to be good at planning, often showing excellent leadership qualities. When control is important in a parenting situation, parents who value control need to focus on controlling the situation and not the child. This can be done by giving choices to the child and letting the child participate in setting limits and determining consequences. (Chapter 7 discusses using consequences.)

Pleasing Others
People who have pleasing as a priority are concerned with approval from others. They can't stand to be rejected. Their beliefs usually include:

1. "I must please others."
2. "I must be liked by everyone all the time."
3. "I must avoid rejection and gain everyone's approval."

Pleasers pay a high price for this priority. In their attempt to please everyone, they can spread themselves too thin. Others frequently take advantage of them. People who try to please may complain of a lack of self-respect and lack of respect from others. They also can develop an ineffective relationship with their children if they work hard to always please the children.

> Marlita did everything she could to please her 15-year-old daughter, Louisa. She constantly sewed outfits for Louisa in the latest styles and gave her large amounts of money to spend on makeup and jewelry. She wanted to be Louisa's "pal," so she never restricted what Louisa could do and always gave in to her demands. Louisa took advantage of Marlita's giving nature, but to Marlita's distress, did not give any love in return.

On the positive side, pleasers are concerned with others. They tend to be friendly, perceptive, understanding, and sensitive. They are usually generous and are good at understanding how their children feel. These parents need to learn most of all to be firm as well as kind. They have to be careful not to let their children take advantage of their desire to please.

Maintaining Comfort
People who put their own comfort first believe they must avoid pain and responsibility. They often hold some of the following beliefs:

1. "I must avoid physical or emotional pain."
2. "I must avoid conflict and stress."
3. "I must avoid responsibility."
4. "I am inadequate."

People who put comfort first frequently do not make full use of their talents. They are not as productive as they might be because to push themselves may be uncomfortable. When they put an emphasis upon their own comfort instead of their children's, they may invite resistance. A parent who is always thinking of herself and her comfort is not in a position to participate in a give-and-take with a child.

> Cheri and her husband, Kenny, were easygoing parents with a good sense of humor but also tended to put their own comfort first. Cheri's two boys and Kenny's girl rarely participated in after-school activities because Cheri and Kenny thought it was too inconvenient to give them rides. Cheri and Kenny only did things with their children if the activities in no way interfered with their leisure time pursuits of visiting friends, playing golf, and watching TV.

The positive side of comfort seekers is that they tend to be easygoing, undemanding parents because they want to keep the peace and avoid conflict. They provoke little rebellion in their children. Parents who are comfort seekers must make an effort to do things with and for their children even if they find doing so is inconvenient or uncomfortable. The following chart summarizes for you the characteristics of the personality priorities.

How Beliefs Affect Emotions

You may sometimes say, "that made me feel . . . " or "he made me feel . . . " You say this because people tend to think of emotions as caused by circumstances outside of themselves. In fact,

Chart 4. Characteristics of Personality Priorities

	Goal	Negative Feelings	Complaints of	Positive Qualities	How Children May Feel	Alternatives for Parents
Being Superior	Be better than others. Prove self more competent, right, or useful than others	Overburdened, uncertain, fear of failure and defeat, relationships in doubt	Running out of time, too much to do, guilt, not sure of relationships with others	Creative, positive outlook	Can't do anything right, not good enough, can't live up to parent's standards, must be superior and perfect	Be more accepting of own mistakes and children's mistakes, model the courage to be imperfect
Controlling	Control others or control self, have own way, be the boss	Fear of humiliation, embarrassment, and ridicule. Cautious of unexpected. Difficulty acknowledging feelings, socially distant	Lacking friends. Not feeling close to others	Well organized, good at planning, leadership qualities	Not safe to share feelings, may stay distant	Focus on controlling situation, not child

Chart 4. Characteristics of Personality Priorities (cont.)

Pleasing Others	Please others, be liked by everyone all of the time, avoid rejection	Spread too thin, taken advantage of, not respected	Lacking self-respect and respect from others	Concerned with others, friendly, perceptive, understanding, sensitive, generous, understanding of children's feelings	Disrespectful, may take advantage of parent	Learn to be firm as well as kind
Maintaining Comfort	Avoid physical or emotional pain, conflict and stress, and responsibility	Inadequacy	Lessened productivity	Easygoing, undemanding	Little participation by parent, not important to parents	Make an effort to do things with and for children even if not convenient

Note. Partially adapted with permission from *Basic Applications of Adlerian Psychology* (p.23) by Edith A. Dewey, 1978, Coral Springs, FL: CMTI Press.

people are not helpless victims of external forces. They decide how they feel, based upon their perceptions and the way they choose to respond.

Emotions give people the strength to act with force and conviction. They provide the capacity to enjoy, to be involved, and to experience the positive feelings of friendships and closeness. However, emotions do not cause behavior. Nor do they dictate to people or control them. Instead, people use emotions to serve their goals and purposes.

When you have an emotional response, you may be puzzled about the strong feeling you are experiencing. You need to ask yourself "Am I experiencing threat?" "Am I concerned about being out of control?" "Am I fearful that things won't go the way I want them to go?" "What am I trying to avoid?" When you understand the context in which the emotion occurs, it will help you to understand that the emotion is purposeful, that it is created to help you attain a goal, and that it is affected by your personality priorities. For example, if you believe people are trustworthy and kind, you may create positive feelings about people that can move you closer to others. If, on the other hand, you think people are out to hurt you or take advantage of you, you may create feelings that keep you at a distance from others.

Becoming more aware of how and why you create strong, upsetting emotions will enable you to determine ways to stop creating them. Albert Ellis and Robert Harper, noted psychologists, have offered an explanation of how people talk themselves into negative feelings.[3] The letters *A, B,* and *C* are used to describe this process.

> *A* stands for the activating event, the thing that happens to the person.
>
> *B* is the person's belief about *A.*
>
> *C* is the emotional consequence of the belief about the activating event.

Many people think that *A* causes *C,* or that the event produces a specific emotional response. For example, if your son challenges your authority and you as a result feel angry, *A,* the activating event, appears to have caused your feelings about yourself.

However, you create your own emotions, and so it is not logical to think that your son caused you to feel angry. *A* cannot make you feel anything. Thus, look instead at *B*, your belief about *A*, the activating event. It is possible that you told yourself, "He has no right to challenge me. Children should always obey their parents." If you told yourself these things, then you might feel angry, and this feeling will interfere with your relationship with your son.

You could tell yourself something different, something more rational, when your son challenges you. You might say instead, "I prefer not to be challenged but I can live with it. My son has to learn to make his own decisions and questioning authority is part of that process. I will be friendly with him and do what I can to establish a positive relationship and will let him be responsible for the way he acts."

People cause their own emotional upsets by thinking of their preferences as needs. You may prefer that something would happen and immediately decide that it *should* happen. This then becomes an irrational belief. These irrational beliefs may lead to "catastrophizing"—making yourself unhappy and ineffective

because you view the things that don't go your way as catastrophies instead of seeing them simply as frustrating or unfortunate. For example, you will be very unhappy if you think your daughter must be homecoming queen and you see her losing as a catastrophe. Trying to command life to be on your terms only leads to misery. Behaving rationally simply means doing the best you can in your relationships and having confidence in your ability to handle any results.

People can also make themselves upset when they begin to feel they are not worthwhile because of the way they are being treated. They may condemn themselves or begin to attack the person who is mistreating them. For example, you will make yourself unhappy if you condemn yourself because your coworker criticizes you. Condemning is irrational. No one's behavior makes you worthless. Everyone has faults and assets. It is rational only to judge behavior, not someone's worth.

Your Emotions and Your Child's Misbehavior Goal

In the previous chapter you learned about the goals of your children's misbehavior and how to respond to them. Now that you know how your beliefs affect your emotions, you can look at what you believe about your children's behavior and understand why you may feel upset by the behavior. When you understand your negative beliefs about the behavior, you can change them to more positive beliefs.

Beliefs about the Goal of Attention

Imagine your child trying to get your attention by being noisy and running through the house. You might find yourself annoyed and you might think, "She should stop this." However, if your child is attempting to get your attention and you are providing attention, there is no logical reason for her to stop.

A more effective belief about attention getting might be, "It would be nice if she would stop distracting me. But, since she won't, I'll ignore her attempts to get my attention." This eliminates your annoyance. You switch to a preference rather than a requirement that the child stop and withdraw your attention from the misbehavior. The responsibility for the behavior is placed on the child. Thus you have new choices about responding that stem from a more effective set of beliefs.

Beliefs about the Goal of Power

When your child seeks power, you often feel angry because you feel challenged. Your belief could be "Children must obey" or "I am a failure if I don't get complete cooperation." If you choose under these circumstances to prove that you are in charge, the purpose of your anger is to regain control. If you decide to give in, you may use anger to get even for losing the battle. If you learn to change your irrational beliefs about power, you will be able to win your child's cooperation by refusing to fight or to give in. You could tell yourself, "It would be nice if he did not challenge me, but even though he continues to challenge me, I do not have to engage in power contests." You may feel frustrated, but you will recognize that your situation is not awful or something that you can't stand. You don't have to let the power struggle affect your feelings of worth as a parent. As you remove yourself from power struggles, you educate your child and model a more effective behavior.

Beliefs about the Goal of Revenge

If your child's goal is revenge, you may think, "There must be something wrong with me, or he wouldn't attack me" or "How could he be so unfair to me?" Your feelings may be hurt and you may get angry and begin to attack your child. You may believe, "I've been treated unfairly and I must get even." A more rational thought would be "It is unfortunate he has treated me this way" or "I would prefer he treated me differently, but I will survive this attack."

Beliefs about the Goal of Display of Inadequacy

If your child displays inadequacy, you may feel despair and use this feeling as an excuse to give up. You may think, "I can't believe that I failed. If I were a more effective parent I would have been able to help. If only I could do something about this." As you recognize that your child acts inadequate to reach a goal, you can free yourself from the tendency to despair. A more rational thought would be "It would be better if he could succeed. I'll try encouraging him more."

Guilt

People's high standards and the expectations of others combine to help produce guilt feelings. Parents only need look around them to see things that they believe they "should" feel guilty about. A parent may choose to feel guilty about a child's poor schoolwork, shyness, size and appearance, or anything at all. A single mother may feel guilty because she thinks she's not nurturing enough now that she's busy supporting the family. A father may feel guilty about leaving his children after a divorce. Stepparents may feel guilty when their attempts at nurturance are rejected by children who do not see them as parents. A couple in a stepfamily may feel guilty because their bond is growing while it appears their children are being "neglected."

Lack of time to spend with children can make single parents feel particularly guilty. Community pressure on single parents to be involved with their children is as great as it is for other families, but the time single parents have available is much less. When single parents feel guilty about not spending time with their children, they teach the children to expect more than other children because they have only one parent and are therefore disadvantaged.

Guilt feelings are very subjective and often are not valid. Guilt feelings are no more unique than any other emotion; they have a purpose and they are created.

Guilt feelings may be the expression of good intentions that people do not have.[4] Guilt seems to express a desire to be good and to behave properly, but it is used to defy order and obligation without admitting such defiance openly.[5] Guilt feelings are sometimes used to get an exemption from having to function. After all, if someone feels guilty, should he also have to do something? The guilt may provide a protection from strong and angry feelings people have about themselves or others. Guilt also is a way of resisting and saying no to life. People can use guilt feelings to stop participating in life. Guilt feelings are eliminated by becoming aware of the purpose of the guilt and taking action to improve the situation.

Guilt feelings provide no growth for the family. Instead they provide an opportunity for children to manipulate the parent. They teach the children to feel sorry for themselves and demand constant reassurance from the parent.

Grief and Stages of the Grieving Process

With divorce or death there will be loss and grief that needs to be worked through. The ending of a marital relationship is a stress both parents and children need to learn to face.

Elizabeth Kübler-Ross has identified the five stages of the grieving process as: denial, anger, bargaining, depression, and acceptance.[6] Whether the loss of a family member is due to death or divorce, it is important to understand these stages of grieving and that everyone goes through them in a unique way and at his own pace.

1. *Denial.* In the first stage of grieving family members believe, "This really can't be happening to us." They deny reality and are unwilling to accept the situation. At this point panic can emerge.

2. *Anger.* The second stage of grieving includes hostility and anger directed at the absent family member and displaced anger aimed at people in general. At this point family members may think, "This can't be happening to us; we haven't done anything wrong" and "How could he do this to us?"

3. *Bargaining.* Stage 3 consists of bargaining, promises to do better if given a second chance. This bargaining is done with the intent to delay the inevitable.

4. *Depression.* The depression experienced by each family member in Stage 4 reflects attempts to cope with unexpected changes in the family resulting from loss. Learning to deal with temporary depression facilitates movement to acceptance of the loss.

5. *Acceptance.* At this stage, each family member has worked through the four previous stages and has come to terms with the loss. They are now ready to move ahead and get on with living.

Even when the loss of a parent is the result of death, children often feel they are somehow at fault. Isolating the children from the dying parent and not allowing them to say good-bye tends to support this faulty belief. In some instances of death or divorce, children may think, "If I only would have been better, this wouldn't have happened." Listen for the children's feelings, don't moralize, and be patient. Everyone goes through the stages of grief at a different pace.

It is important to resolve differences with your ex-spouse privately to reduce children's grief and stress. Do not encourage children to take sides. Fighting and disagreeing in front of the children, or reporting the content of arguments, will only encourage the children to attempt to manipulate the relationship. More on resolving conflicts with your ex-spouse can be found in Chapter 8.

Stress

Stress is the physical and emotional response that people experience when they perceive an event as upsetting. Many events have the potential for stress. It is not the event itself, but a person's perceptions and interpretation that cause stress.[7]

The same events do not produce stress for everyone. For example, some people are stressed if called upon to make a public presentation of any kind or to handle a family conflict. Public presentations stimulate other people, however, to perform more effectively, and family conflicts give some people an opportunity to utilize skills.

You have the opportunity to decide how to see any given event and can choose to experience situations as challenging instead of stressful. You also can learn how to control and alter your physical and emotional responses. It is possible to learn a relaxation procedure and choose a less stressful way of thinking about your experiences.

Thinking in absolutes and focusing on *must, should,* and *have to* can bring on stress. You can learn to dispute your irrational beliefs. Suppose you've made a mistake and have behaved inappropriately with your children. You could say, "I'm so stupid and worthless. How could I have done that?" Or, you could choose to say, "That was a mistake. It's unfortunate, but I can accept it. It would be better if things went perfectly, but that's not realistic and a mistake doesn't make me a bad parent." Then you can choose a belief that leads to a more constructive way of dealing with situations. Remind yourself that you can decide what you think and how you are going to behave.

It's important for both parents and children to learn to relax. Tension and anxiety actually diminish when you relax. You replace fear with a sense of peace and well-being. Relaxation, then, overcomes the effects of stress. When you are relaxed your heart rate becomes slower, your breathing becomes deeper, and your muscles loosen and relax. Relaxation energizes you, leaving you ready to get involved with your work, your interests, and your relationships. While it takes a certain amount of time and practice to learn to create a state of relaxation, some very simple exercises can help you to relax any time, any place.

Deep breathing is probably the simplest of all the relaxation procedures. When a person experiences stress, his breathing often becomes shallow and rapid. However, when he relaxes, his breathing will become deeper and slower. If you take just 30 to 40 seconds to practice deep breathing, you can help reduce the effects of stress you may be feeling.

You can learn to relax by sitting back in a comfortable chair, breathing in and out, slowly and deeply but naturally. You might push out your stomach each time you breathe out. As you breathe in and out, you will begin to feel the tension drain from your body. If you practice deep breathing on a daily basis, it will become a resource for you to combat any form of stress. Herbert Benson's book, *Beyond the Relaxation Response*,[8] and Edward Charlesworth and Ronald Nathan's book, *Stress Management*,[9] are among the books available that give relaxation exercises.

Acceptance of the unique personality and emotions of each family member provides the foundation for self-esteem and open communication in the family. Your understanding how people create their own emotions will help you to use the tools of communication presented in the next chapter.

Activity Assignment

During the next week, become aware of how your personality priorities affect your parenting and take steps to change the priorities.

Important Points to Remember in Chapter 4

1. Heredity, family atmosphere and values, and family constellation influence the development of a child's personality and lifestyle.

2. Parents need to explore values with children, not impose their values on children.

3. A child's position in the family constellation accounts for many of the differences between the child and siblings.

4. Personality priorities influence our relationships. Four common personality priorities are:

- To be superior
- To be in control
- To please others
- To maintain your own comfort

5. The healthiest personality priority is social interest, or to cooperate with others to further society's interest.

6. Emotions serve people's goals and purposes. You can understand your emotions by recognizing:

A—the activating event
B—your belief about A
C—the emotional consequence of your belief about the activating event

7. People cause their emotional upsets by thinking of their preferences as needs.

8. If you understand your beliefs about your child's goal of misbehavior, you can change your feelings and the way you react to the misbehavior.

9. Guilt serves the purpose of defying obligation, protecting from strong emotions, and saying no to life.

10. After a divorce or death, all family members need an opportunity to go through the stages of grief—denial, anger, bargaining, depression, and acceptance.

11. Stress can be handled by changing your belief about the stressful event and using simple relaxation techniques.

Chapter 5

Communication Skills

When someone really listens to you, how do you feel? It's quite likely you feel cared about. Taking the time to really listen to people and to try to understand what they are saying shows that you value them. Similarly, being open and honest with your feelings demonstrates the same thing. Respectfully telling people how you feel about their behavior when it bothers you shows confidence in their ability to accept and respond to your feelings. Sharing your positive feelings shows you care.

Many feelings are associated with a change in the family structure. Children in single-parent families and stepfamilies experience all the feelings involved in growing up as do children in nuclear families. In addition, they feel loss, anger about their family situation, and fear of abandonment. It's especially important, then, for parents in single-parent families and stepfamilies to develop skills for listening to and dealing with their children's feelings. It is also important for parents to be able to effectively communicate their feelings about how the children's behavior affects them.

How can you communicate effectively when faced with a child's problem or one of your own? Communication skills are seldom taught. People learn to communicate simply by observation. The problem with this approach is that people often pick up some ineffective skills without realizing it. For example, parents often wonder why their children don't listen when they tell the children the same thing over and over again. The parents don't realize that the children have heard what has been said and have simply chosen not to listen. When children express upset feelings, what do most parents do? They may lecture, question, threaten, judge, give advice, criticize, pity, or reassure.

These responses are "turn-offs." When people express their upset feelings, they often want others to simply listen and try to understand. Children are no different. When parents lecture, advise, or judge, they rob children of the opportunity to be heard. When parents pity or reassure, they communicate to children that the children cannot handle a situation, and they deny the children's feelings.

The way parents communicate their feelings about children's behavior also can turn off the children. Many parents tend to threaten, criticize, judge, or plead when their children's behavior bothers them. Children tend to ignore, rebel, get even, or become discouraged when parents communicate in these ways. Both verbal and nonverbal communication can affect how children respond to their parents' messages.

Effective communication is based on mutual respect. When parents demonstrate respect to their children, chances are the children will return that respect. Effective communicators tune into a person's feelings and opinions. They clearly state what they feel and believe in nonthreatening ways.

This chapter will focus on effective ways to listen to and talk to your children. The suggestions in the chapter may seem uncomfortable and strange to both you and your children at first. Like any new skill, such as learning to drive, these approaches will be awkward in the beginning. With practice, they can become more natural and personalized.

Problem Ownership

Effective responses to parent-child problems depend on the goal of the child in the problem and who owns the problem. Who owns a problem refers to who is responsible for handling a situation.[1] For example, if a parent is trying to watch a favorite TV show and the children are in the same room laughing and teasing each other, the parent has a problem: how to call a halt to the behavior so the parent can enjoy the show. The children are not concerned about the interruption; they may simply want the parent's attention. The fact that the parent is busy is the parent's problem. The parent has to handle the situation. On the other hand, if a child is having difficulties with a friend, the child owns the problem. The child's problem with the friend in no way affects the parent or interferes with the parent's rights as a person. It's up to the child to handle the problem (unless there is danger to the child or someone else).

You can determine who owns a problem by asking yourself these questions when something happens.

1. Who does this problem really affect?
2. Who is having a problem with whom?
3. Whose responsibility is it to take care of this problem?

Problems that you own involve your responsibilities as a parent or your rights as a person. All other problems belong to the child. For example, if your child is doing something that jeopardizes her safety or someone else's safety, then you own this problem. But if the child is experiencing a problem in her life that does not affect her basic welfare, then she owns the prob-

"Wait a second. Whose problem is this anyway?"

lem. The following example shows how a problem can affect your rights as a person.

> Elena, age 11, has been taking piano lessons. Lately she has shown a lack of interest, and her teacher has complained to Elena's father, Matthew. At first glance the problem seems to be between Elena and her teacher; yet since Matthew is paying for the lessons, the problem actually belongs to him. Matthew's rights are being violated because he's doling out money and Elena is not practicing. Matthew could just stop paying for the lessons and decide to transfer ownership of the problem to Elena by having her earn the money for the lessons if she really wants to continue them.

Some parents insist on being involved with all of their children's problems. They settle arguments, conflicts with the children and the other parent, and disputes with the teacher. They make sure that homework is done and that the children are never hungry—even if they refuse to eat dinner—and so on. When parents take over the children's problems, they teach them to be dependent. While this may help the parent feel worthwhile through being superior, it handicaps the children.

If a child owns a problem, a parent can choose either to listen and help the child find her own solution or let the child face the consequences on her own. For example, if a child has a problem with a friend and expresses concern to the parent, the parent can listen to the child and help the child decide how to deal with the situation. If the child refuses to wear a coat and becomes cold, the parent can let the child deal with being cold.

When a parent owns the problem, she can choose either to let the children know how she feels about it or use a logical consequence (see Chapter 7). For example, if the children are misbehaving while the parent is trying to watch TV, the parent could respectfully point out to the children that they are disturbing her or give them a choice of settling down and watching the program with her or leaving the room. Allowing children to settle their own problems—and taking care of your own—models respect and problem solving.

Nonverbal Communication

Good communication involves more than the words that some-one says. Feelings and meanings are communicated by body language and tone of voice, as well as by words.

Body Language

Facial expressions, posture, movement, and eye contact all convey feelings. Have you ever talked to someone who claims she's not upset, and yet she is frowning and has a tear in her eye? Her body language tells her real feelings, even though her words may be different.

Much of human communication is nonverbal. Therefore, it is especially important for parents to be aware of their children's body language. For example, does a child appear nervous or calm when she talks to you? Do her hands and legs tremble, or does she sit in a quiet, relaxed way? Does she fidget and look away, or does she look you in the eyes when she speaks? These different nonverbal clues can give you an idea about how she is feeling.

There are no hard, fixed rules about interpreting body language, only probabilities. For example, arms crossed on the chest often mean a person is defensive, but not always. For some people, this is simply a relaxed posture. Putting clues together helps you be more accurate. Crossed arms coupled with clenched teeth and a rigid posture, for example, give you a pretty strong clue to the person's defensiveness.

To see if what you notice from body language is correct, check it out. If your child is acting in a nervous way you could say, "You seem nervous." If the child denies the feeling but continues to act in the same way, you could point out to the child that her words say one thing and her body says another. Then you could ask the child if her words or her body is communicating her real feelings. This will usually produce a clear picture of how the child feels.

When you listen or talk to your children, be aware of what your body may be communicating. As you listen, lean forward, make eye contact without staring, and have a relaxed posture. When you communicate your feelings, make sure your expressions are as respectful as your words.

Tone of Voice

If a person's tone of voice doesn't match his words, chances are the real feelings are being communicated by the tone of voice. For example, if your son tells you everything is OK with a shaking or angry voice, things probably are not OK.

Watch your tone of voice when you speak to your children. If your words are friendly but your tone is hostile, the child will hear the feelings expressed by your tone of voice.

Accurate communication involves attention to body language, tone of voice, and choice of words. If the nonverbal clues and the tone of voice don't match the words being expressed, the child will ignore the words.

Connie, age 5, is upset about breaking her favorite toy. She comes crying to her mother, Becky, who is busy working on papers she's brought home from the office. Without looking at Connie, Becky flatly says, "I see you're sad about breaking your toy." Through her tears, Connie asks, "Can I get another one, Mommy?" Becky answers, "We'll see." Connie whimpers for a while then sadly walks away leaving Becky to her work.

It's obvious Connie did not feel understood. Becky decided her work was more important than the few minutes it would have taken to deal with Connie's feelings.

Listening for Your Children's Feelings

Feelings, like goals, affect behavior. Helping children deal with their feelings often produces behavior change. Children send parents feeling messages every day. Often, parents don't take time to listen or don't know how to respond.

There are several ways to listen to children and demonstrate caring and respect. Sometimes, simply remaining silent and attentive is all that is needed. At other times, parents need to show children that they recognize how the children feel. Simple statements like "I see," "I understand," or "I'm with you" show parents are listening.

There are many times, however, when parents need to respond in a way that demonstrates that they really understand what children are trying to communicate. An effective way to show this understanding is to use a skill called *reflective listening*.

Reflective Listening

Reflective listening involves making a statement in your own words that communicates you understand another's feelings and the facts associated with the feelings. For example, imagine your son comes home from school and says, "I really blew it today. The teacher asked me a question. I didn't know the answer, and the whole class laughed at me!" Chances are this child is feeling very embarrassed. You could simply respond, "It seems you were very embarrassed because the class made fun of you." By making this response, you've shown your son you understand what he's feeling and the circumstances, or facts, that led to the feeling. It's quite likely he will appreciate your concern and understanding.

Contrast the response just mentioned with more typical responses by parents: "Well, you will need to study harder next time" or "Don't worry about it; I'm sure the other kids get laughed at, too" or "Why didn't you know the answer?" How might your son feel about you if you gave one of these responses?

The first response, "It seems you were very embarrassed," is an example of an *open* response. An open response is a statement that communicates in your own words that you have understood what the child is trying to say. Children seldom communicate by using feeling words. They often don't know appropriate words for feelings because these words are not taught to them. By making open, reflective listening responses, you can "decode" what a child is trying to say and show that you really understand and care about the child's feelings. Also, you model appropriate ways to communicate feelings and teach the child to express feelings directly through using these words yourself.

Responses such as "Well, you'll need to study harder next time" are examples of *closed* responses. Closed responses often involve lectures, commands, advice, judgments, and denial of feelings. These responses turn off the child.

Using Reflective Listening

Suppose a child said to her father, "Mom's so unfair! She makes us go to bed at 9:00!" How could he use reflective listening to respond to her? First he would think of what feeling is being expressed. In this case, the feeling is probably anger. Next he would think of the facts of the situation. Here the situation is that the mother makes the daughter go to bed early. Then he could respond to the feeling and the fact by saying something such as "You're angry because Mom makes you go to bed early."

There are several ways to phrase a reflective listening response. When you are first beginning, you may want to use the simple response statement "You feel _____ because _____" and just "fill in the blanks." Here are some examples of reflective listening responses.

Child's Statement: "Boy, are we going to have fun this summer! Mom's friend is letting us use her cabin at the lake for 2 weeks!"

Feeling: Excitment.

Fact: The child is going to the lake.

Reflective Listening Response: "You feel excited because you're going to the lake this summer."

Child's Statement: "Dad told me he's going to get married. She has three kids who are going to live with them. What will happen to me?"

Feeling: Worry.

Fact: The child might be replaced by the stepmother's three children.

Reflective Listening Response: "You feel worried because you think her three children might replace you in your dad's heart."

The first example is straightforward and easy to understand. The second example has a hidden concern—losing a place in the new family. Some feeling messages have hidden concerns, especially if they are stated in question form.

As you learn to make reflective listening responses, the wording will become easier. Here are some other ways to phrase your response to the child's feelings.

> "You're feeling ———— ."
> "You sound ———— ."
> "It seems to me you're feeling ———— ."
> "Is this the way you're feeling?"

You can respond to the facts associated with the feeling by substituting *when, with, at, by,* or *about* for the *because* statement in "You feel ———— because ———— ."

Refrain from using the statement "You feel that . . . " unless you're reflecting the child's opinion. "You feel that" does not reflect feelings. For example, suppose your child is complaining about mistreatment by his friends. If you said, "You feel that people should be nice to each other," you would be reflecting the child's opinion, not his feelings.

When you reflect your child's feelings, you are making your best guess as to what the child is feeling. As you listen, ask yourself what the child might be feeling and why and then put your idea into words. Remember, you are making a guess, not telling the child what he feels. Therefore, be tentative in responding to the child. Your comments, tone, and nonverbal behavior can communicate to the child that you are checking out a guess.

Reflective listening involves capturing the child's feelings and meanings, not interpreting. Interpreting involves giving your own opinion—what the child's statement means to you. While you may be correct, interpreting often leaves the child feeling analyzed rather than understood. Here's an example of the difference between reflecting and interpreting.

Child's Statement: (Child slams door as she comes in and is crying.) "I was playing with Marcia and Judy came up and told me to get out of there, or she would beat me up!"

Reflective Listening Response: "Sounds like you're mad because Judy bullied you."

Interpretative Response: "Sounds like you were afraid you would get hurt if you didn't do what Judy said."

Reflecting Feelings Accurately
To be effective, it's important that reflective listening responses be interchangeable with what the child is attempting to communicate. In their desire to be understanding, parents may occasionally magnify the feeling expressed by their children and miss the point.

> Ricky complained to his dad, Harris, about how a friend had treated him. Harris reflected what he thought Ricky was feeling by saying, "You're very angry with her for ignoring you." Ricky replied, "No, I'm not real mad at her. I just didn't like what she did, that's all." Harris "overshot the mark," but Ricky sensed his attempt to understand.

Underemphasizing a feeling can sometimes be a problem because the child may feel you don't understand or care. While it's best to match the child's feelings, overemphasizing a feeling is better than underemphasizing it. Using adverbs helps pick up on intense feelings. *Very, pretty*, and *really* are useful words to have in your feeling vocabulary.

If you have difficulty picking up on a child's feelings, here are some things you can do.

1. Be attentive, but remain silent until you've got a clue to the feeling.

2. Tell the child you are having difficulty understanding and ask him to tell you again how he feels.

3. Use summary feedback instead of immediate feedback. Let the child pour out all of his feelings and then say something like "Let me see if I understand how you feel. From what you told me, it seems you are feeling _____ ." Summary feedback is also very useful when the child is very upset and you don't want to interrupt.

4. Respond to an incomplete message and ask for more information. You could say something such as "Sounds as though you're very hurt. What exactly did happen?" If the child begins to tell you the facts of the situation, your response can then be more complete. If not, ask the child to tell you about the problem.

Sometimes children will be silent after they share a feeling and you've reflected it. Avoid jumping in to start the conversation again. Silence often means the child is thinking about your response. If the silence persists, you can make a statement about what you think is going on: "Looks as though you're unhappy with my response."

Parents often wonder what to do after they reflect a feeling and the child acknowledges he has understood. Some children will be satisfied with your response and stop sharing. Others will open up. When the child opens up, he will often give you additional feelings associated with the situation. Tune in on these feelings and reflect them. When the child seems calmed down—often after two or three reflective statements from you—you can usually help the child solve the problem through a process called exploring alternatives discussed in Chapter 6.

Some parents avoid reflective listening because they are afraid they'll make a mistake. Trying to be perfect is as much a problem in using listening skills as it is in any other aspect of life. If you are sincere and communicate you really want to understand, children will appreciate the effort.

Communicating Your Feelings to Your Children

There are basically two ways parents communicate their feelings to their children: they send either *You-messages* or *I-messages*.[2] You-messages are put-downs of children. They blame, criticize, ridicule, and judge. For example, the You-message "You're so rude. Must you constantly interrupt me?" labels the child and certainly doesn't invite cooperation.

I-messages simply share how you feel about the consequences a child's behavior produces for you. When parents send I-messages, they take responsibility for their own feelings instead of blaming the child for their feelings. For example, the parent who is interrupted could respectfully say, "When I'm interrupted, I feel discouraged because it seems my opinion is not important." In this way the parent simply shares what she is experiencing, rather than engaging in name calling and blame. The child is, thus, more encouraged to listen and respect the parent's feelings. Notice that the parent does not suggest what the child do about the behavior that is interfering with the parent. Instead, the parent trusts the child to respond positively.

You-messages tend to reinforce the child's misbehavior goals because the parent is responding in an expected manner. I-messages, on the other hand, are often unexpected because the parent is simply expressing her own feelings rather than criticizing the child. The unexpected I-message will "defuse" the child's goal.

Taking responsibility for your feelings means you avoid phrases such as "you make me feel." This phrase implies that the child is responsible for your feelings. As you learned in Chapter 4, you are responsible for your own feelings—no one can make another person feel a certain way.

Here are some examples of situations for which I-messages would be appropriate. Notice the difference in phrasing between the You-message examples and the I-messages.

Situation: Child is late when parent picks him up during visitation time.

You-message: "Why are you always late? Now get dressed so we can go!"

I-message: "When you're not ready to be picked up, I feel disappointed because our time together is short, and I want to be with you as much as I can."

Situation: Child yells at parent.

You-message: "Don't you dare yell at me! You better show some respect!"

I-message: "I can see you're angry (acknowledging child's feelings), but when I'm yelled at I feel put down because I'm not respected."

Notice the respect in the I-messages. Put yourself in the child's place. Which messages would stand a better chance of influencing you?

Phrasing I-Messages

I-messages judge behavior and how you feel about it rather than judging the child. Also, I-messages stress how the behavior affects you. If a child's behavior does not interfere with your rights or wants, there is no appropriate reason for you to be upset about it. For example, if your children are playing baseball in the yard away from house windows, their behavior would not be a problem. However, if they are playing near the windows, you have reason to be concerned. I-messages usually consist of three parts.[3]

1. A statement describing the behavior you find trouble-some (describe the behavior without placing blame): "When I find the milk left on the counter . . . "
2. A statement describing your feelings about the results of the misbehavior: "I feel concerned . . . "
3. A statement describing the results of the behavior: ". . . because it might spoil."

I-messages can be phrased by using the format: "When _____ , I feel _____ because _____ ." For example, "When I find the milk left on the counter, I feel concerned because it might spoil."

Since You-messages often contain the word *you*, it is important to make every effort to keep the word *you* out of your I-messages so they won't be interpreted as You-messages. Whenever possible, use phrases like "when I find," "when I see," or "when (such and such) happens." Sometimes the word *you* cannot be avoided, such as in the phrase "when you're not ready." If you have to use the word *you*, be careful not to come across in a blaming way.

In addition to your choice of words, watch your tone of voi·e and body language. To be effective with I-messages, you must demonstrate respect. I-messages aren't magical solutions to problems; they are simply a means to improve your chances of gaining cooperation.

Avoiding Angry Messages

When parents first learn about I-messages, some use them as a means to vent their anger at their children. Angry messages are just You-messages said in a different way. When parents send hostile messages, it is very difficult for children to interpret them as nonthreatening. Children often become defensive and shoot hostile messages back at the parents, and the war is on!

When you feel angry, search for the feelings that led to the anger. Often there are other, nonhostile feelings, like disappointment, fear, and embarrassment, which were not expressed. These feelings, left unexpressed, can build up to anger. If you express these other feelings in nonblaming, respectful ways, you will find you are more effective than when blasting the child with hostile feelings.

Of course, people do slip and get angry at times. Occasional anger is usually not a problem—it "clears the air." However, many parents frequently experience anger. Frequent angry or hurt feelings indicate a problem in the relationship. The anger serves the purpose of controlling, winning, or getting even. If you find yourself frequently angry, search for the purpose of your anger and evaluate the effectiveness of your communication. Perhaps you need to go off by yourself when you feel angry, calm down, and then talk with your children.

Guidelines for Effective Communication

The following guidelines will help you put your new communication skills into action. Communication skills, like any new skill, take time, practice, and patience with yourself and your children.

Invite Conversation

Often your children will not begin a conversation with you about their feelings. You need to be on the alert for nonverbal messages. You may notice a frown, a tear, an angry expression, or an excited, happy look. You can open a conversation by making a comment about what you are observing: "You seem sad." "You look angry. Want to tell me about it?" Sometimes the child will deny a feeling: "No, I'm just tired." If this happens, simply accept the child's comment. There will be other opportunities to share feelings.

Take the time to ask your children to share their feelings, opinions, and beliefs about family issues, current events, and their own interests. The talks don't need to be counseling sessions; you can talk about any subject you both are interested in. "How do you feel about it?" and "What do you think about this?" are good ways to start meaningful conversations. An answer of "fine," "okay," or "I don't know" may indicate the child would rather not share. It's best not to probe, but you can show an interest at another time. Sometimes children will jump at the opportunity to share their feelings as in the following example.

Parent:	How did the game go today?
Child:	Terrible! We were winning by a mile and the coach still wouldn't let me play!
Parent:	So, you're pretty mad at the coach for leaving you on the bench.
Child:	Yeah. I mean, I know I'm not that good, but he could have given me a chance with us winning and all.
Parent:	Sounds like you're pretty discouraged because he won't even give you a chance when the team's winning.
Child:	Yeah. I might as well quit. It's not fun sitting out every game on the bench!

Here the parent has given the child an opportunity to share feelings. This type of discussion could lead to problem solving. The parent and child could discuss ways the child could talk with the coach or perhaps join another activity if this one continued to be unsatisfactory to the child.

Make Time to Listen
There are times when a child wants to talk and you are involved in other things, such as rushing to keep an appointment or

talking with someone else. When you can't listen to the child at the moment, tell the child you really want to listen, state your problem, and set up a time to talk. Delaying some conversations is a fact of life and teaches mutual respect. But, unfortunately, some parents are seldom available when children want to talk. Lack of availability teaches children their concerns don't count. When possible, be available when your child wants to talk.

Avoid Trying to Force Children to Share

When attempting to get children to discuss feelings, consider your attempt an invitation rather than a demand. If you inquire about a child's feelings or make a reflective statement and the child doesn't want to talk, accept the child's response. Feelings are personal and to be respected. Most children will share their feelings if parents are patient and accepting. Some children do not share feelings no matter what the parent does. This simply means that sharing of feelings violates the child's belief system and does not indicate parental failure.

Model Sharing Feelings

Since children often don't know how to share their feelings, you can model appropriate ways of doing this. Share how things are going in your life (but not in areas beyond the child's ability to cope—such as a love relationship). Suppose you are concerned about a friend who is in the hospital. You could say to your child "I'm worried about my friend's operation." Or, suppose something exciting happened at work. You might say, "I really had a great day today."

Like most adults, most children don't know how to communicate their feelings when someone's actions are interfering with their rights. Sending I-messages in a firm but respectful way models how to send feelings about someone's behavior.

Reflect and Express Pleasant Feelings

Life is not all gloom and doom. Positive feelings are important too. Notice and comment on your children's happiness and excitement. Recognizing joy shows interest and caring too.

Also, communicate your positive feelings toward the child: "I appreciated your help at dinner." "Thanks for being ready when

"And so I said to my boss, 'Mr. Webster,
when you say that, I feel . . .'"

I came to pick you up. I really enjoy my time with you." Expressing positive feelings builds relationships and self-esteem.

Experiment with Communication Skills

Reflective listening and I-messages are new ways of communicating that may seem strange to both you and your children at
first. You may not get the response you want the first few times
you use these skills. But do give them a fair test. Use the "formu-
las" mentioned earlier when you first begin using these skills.
Eventually you'll develop your own personal style of responding
to and communicating feelings. The following chart gives you
some examples of how to use communication skills when the
child owns the problem and when the parent owns the problem.

Also, watch your vocabulary. Use words for feelings you are
comfortable with and that your child will understand. Eventually you can expand your child's feeling word vocabulary by

Chart 5. Examples of Using Communication Skills for Parent-Owned and Child-Owned Problems

Problem	Who Owns It?	Communication Skill
Child complains about stepparent yelling at him.	Child	Reflective Listening: "You're hurt because Bob yelled at you."
Agreement is child will leave note if she leaves house before parent gets home from work. Child violates agreement.	Parent	I-message: "When I came home and found you were not here and there was no note, I got really scared because I didn't know where you were and thought something happened to you."
Child complains she can have certain privileges in noncustodial parent's house that custodial parent doesn't allow.	Child	Reflective Listening: "You seem pretty disappointed because I don't permit that here."
Children leave kitchen in mess after making snacks.	Parent	I-message: "When I find crumbs on the kitchen counter after I've cleaned up the kitchen, I feel discouraged because it seems my effort was wasted."

using synonyms. Use the Feeling Words Exercise at the end of the chapter as a guide.

When you send I-messages, your children may respond by sending their own I-messages. Be prepared to switch to reflective listening when this happens. In the following example, Joan has asked her children to help her clean out the garage, and they have turned her down, saying they've got other things to do. Notice how she responds to their I-messages.

Joan: When I need some help and am turned down, I feel discouraged because it's a big job and would be done much sooner if we all pitched in.

Kristin: Ah, come on, Mom, I've got enough to do around here.

Jenny: Yeah. Me too!

> Joan: I can see you're upset because I'm asking you to
> take on some extra work. I feel overloaded, too.
> How can we work this out so we can all have some
> time off from chores?

Here the parent stated how she feels about the girls' turning
her down and reflected their feelings. She stated her feelings
about having too much to do herself and paved the way for
problem solving.

Avoid Asking too Many Questions

Sometimes parents ask so many questions that children feel as
though they are being interrogated. Parents may ask questions
because they don't know what else to do. Reflective listening
provides an effective alternative to overuse of questions. Here
are some guidelines for using questions.

1. Ask questions only to get information you actually need
to understand and help. Sometimes people ask unnecessary
questions because the answers may be interesting. Whether or
not information is interesting has no bearing on whether the
information is actually needed. Before you ask the child a question, ask yourself "Do I really need this information?"

2. Don't ask a question when you can make a reflective
response. If a child gives you a feeling message, make a statement about what you think the child is feeling, rather than
asking her how she feels.

3. Keep your questions *open ended*, rather than asking questions that have yes or no for the answer and that limit conversation. For example, some open-ended questions are "What did he
do then?" or "How did you feel when he did that?"

Avoid Overdoing Reflective Listening and I-Messages

Reflective listening is a skill designed to demonstrate understanding and caring. Children will see parents' listening attempts
as meaningless and gimmicky if parents respond to every verbal
and nonverbal expression.

If children ask simple, straightforward questions, such as
"What time will Dad pick me up?" resist the temptation to

respond "You're feeling anxious" and simply answer the question. Of course, if there seems to be concern and upset behind a question or statement, reflective listening is appropriate.

I-messages can also be overdone. Stating your feelings each time children displease you can influence them to ignore your feelings. The children may expect you to make a comment and this could reinforce the goal of their misbehavior. I-messages are only one way to handle parent-owned problems. By experimenting, you'll know when and if to use them.

Reflective listening and I-messages can also reinforce misbehavior goals if they are used inappropriately. For example, when parents start listening, some children discover having and sharing problems is a good way to get attention. If you find your child is sharing the same problem over and over again with no effort to improve the situation, it's quite likely the child has found a negative way to gain attention. Some children seem to come up with one problem after another to talk about with parents. If you find yourself feeling continually annoyed when your child brings up concerns, you may be involved in giving inappropriate attention.

If your child is using problems simply to grab your attention, it's time to back off. Tell the child you are confident she can handle the situation and turn your attention to other tasks. Be sure to replace the attention you take away with positive attention given when the child does not expect it.

Sometimes reflective listening can invite a power contest. If your child is angry with you, reflective listening may make things worse. You may find it difficult to remain calm and matter-of-fact. So, depending on your level of comfort and your child's response, you may decide it is best to tell the child you can see she is angry and think it would be best to discuss the problem when both of you calm down. Then you can take yourself out of the situation.

Good relationships take time to develop and need to be continually nourished through listening and sharing feelings. Remember that listening and sharing feelings appropriately shows caring and respect for your child. Such respectful communication is vital to the decision-making process discussed next.

Activity Assignment

During the next week, practice reflective listening and I-messages with your children and / or stepchildren.

Important Points to Remember in Chapter 5

1. Effective communication is based on mutual respect.

2. Effective responses to parent-child problems depend on the goal of the child and who owns the problem. You can decide if you own a problem by asking yourself:

- Who does the problem really affect?
- Who is having a problem with whom?
- Whose responsibility is it to take care of this problem?

3. Feelings and meanings are communicated by body language and tone of voice as well as by words.

4. Listening demonstrates caring and respect. Reflective listening communicates that you understand another's feelings and the facts associated with the feelings.

5. A reflective listening response can be phrased "You feel _____ because _____."

6. Reflective listening involves presenting the feelings you hear, not interpreting by giving your own opinion about the person's statement.

7. It is better to overemphasize a feeling when you reflect it than to underemphasize a feeling. If you can't pick up on the child's feelings, respond to what you hear and ask for more information.

8. Parents communicate their feelings to their children through You-messages or I-messages. You-messages blame, criticize, ridicule, or judge. I-messages share how parents feel about the consequences a child's behavior produces for them.

9. I-messages involve:

- A statement describing the behavior you find troublesome
- A statement describing your feelings about the results of the misbehavior
- A statement describing the results of the behavior

10. An I-message can be phrased using this format: "When _____, I feel _____ because _____."

11. If you find yourself frequently angry, search for the purpose of your anger and evaluate the effectiveness of your communication.

12. The guidelines for communicating effectively are:

- Invite conversation
- Make time to listen
- Avoid trying to force children to share
- Model sharing feelings
- Reflect and express pleasant feelings
- Experiment with communication skills
- Avoid asking too many questions
- Avoid overdoing reflective listening and I-messages

Feeling Words Exercise

Below is a list of feeling words. See if you can find synonyms and add to the list. Be careful with the use of the word *upset*. This is a "catch all" word that may not convey the depth of a feeling.

Notice each feeling word is paired with an opposite. As you think of a synonym for the first feeling word, see if you can come up with an opposite, such as *happy—sad*, and you will have a synonym for the second word. The more word pairs you can generate, the wider choice of words you will have to use with your children.

accepted _____	rejected _____
afraid _____	safe _____
angry _____	content _____
annoyed _____	accepting _____
appreciated _____	ignored _____
bad _____	good _____
bored _____	excited _____
bothered _____	indifferent _____
brave _____	scared _____
comfortable _____	stressed _____
confused _____	certain _____
defeated _____	successful _____
determined _____	undecided _____
disappointed _____	OK _____
discouraged _____	encouraged _____
disrespected _____	respected _____
down _____	up _____
embarrassed _____	proud _____
foolish _____	confident _____
guilty _____	satisfied _____
happy _____	sad _____
hurt _____	loved _____

interested _____	turned off _____
nervous _____	relaxed _____
pleased _____	irritated _____
proud _____	ashamed _____
surprised _____	shocked _____
trusted _____	doubted _____

Chapter 6

Decision Making

While all families need to learn how to resolve problems and make decisions together, it's especially important for single-parent families and stepfamilies. Members of these family structures face challenges common to all families, plus those unique to their situations. In Chapter 5 you learned about the communication skills of reflective listening and I-messages. This chapter will discuss how to use these skills and a process called exploring alternatives to resolve conflicts and to help children learn to make decisions about the problems they face. Particularly important to decision making and problem solving, as you will see later, is the family meeting.

Exploring Alternatives

Exploring alternatives is a process used to help children resolve problems and used to negotiate parent-child and family conflicts. Problems and conflicts occur in all relationships. A constructive decision-making process to deal with them helps gain cooperation and provides a problem-solving model for children. Exploring alternatives involves the five *Ps* of problem solving.

> Perceive the problem.
> Propose ideas.
> Pick an idea.
> Put the idea into action.
> Plan a time for evaluation.

These five steps can be used to explore alternatives when the child owns the problem, when the parent owns the problem, or in the family meeting—a forum for decision making involving all family members.

Exploring Alternatives for Child-Owned Problems

When a child owns a problem, the child may share it with you. Reflective listening may be all that's needed in some cases. Often, however, the child needs help in solving the problem. The parent doesn't handle the problem for the child but instead helps the child explore alternative ways to solve the problem. The following illustrates the steps used to help a child solve a problem.

1. *Perceive the Problem.* In this step, you help the child feel understood and explore the nature of the problem. You want to understand the feelings and the facts. Use reflective listening to help clarify feelings, beliefs, and issues. If necessary, ask open-ended questions—what, when, where, how—to obtain essential information. You may have to use this step more than once in the discussion if things need to be clarified.

2. *Propose Ideas.* In this step, you encourage the child to make her own suggestions on how to solve the problem. Giving advice is inappropriate, and the advice may not be taken. By helping the child seek her own solutions, you stimulate problem-solving skills.

Use the technique of *brainstorming* in this step to stimulate the creative flow of ideas. Tell the child "Let's brainstorm some ideas you can use to solve this problem. Think of everything you can, even if some of your ideas seem silly. I'll list them and we'll talk about them when you're through. Just say anything that comes to mind. OK. What's your first idea?"

Don't evaluate the ideas until the child has exhausted her possibilities. Evaluating ideas immediately after they are given blocks creativity. Also, sometimes one idea that may seem inappropriate can lead to an appropriate idea when the atmosphere is encouraging.

If the child has trouble thinking of ideas, ask her to pretend the problem is happening to a friend. What would she tell the friend to do? If the child is totally blocked, make a suggestion, but do this as a last resort and phrase it tentatively: "Have you thought of . . . ?" "What would happen if . . . ?"

The results of brainstorming are often impressive.

3. *Pick an Idea.* Ask the child to decide which idea, or combination of ideas, she thinks will work best for her. Begin the process by evaluating each idea. "The first idea you had was _____. What do you think about it?" You may see an aspect of an idea the child does not see. If so, give your opinion, but make sure the child understands it's your opinion and not the "absolute truth": "It seems to me . . . "

Once ideas have been evaluated, ask the child which one she thinks will work the best. Remember this is the child's problem. Don't interfere with her decision unless you think the consequences of the decision will be dangerous.

4. *Put the Idea into Action.* Many children will say they will "try" something but trying doesn't necessarily equal doing! When most people say they will try something, it means they are not sure the idea will work or don't want to use the idea but want you to stop bothering them. Many plans fail because there

is no commitment or time limit. Ask the child if she is willing to experiment with the idea for a certain time period. Often a week is a good test period, or with young children, a day or two may be appropriate. Some things, of course, may need a longer test period.

5. *Plan a Time for Evaluation.* After the commitment is made and the time period set, pick a time with the child to evaluate the plan: "How about talking over how this is going Thursday after dinner?" If the child complains about the plan before the evaluation time, gently remind the child she agreed to experiment with the plan until the set time to see if it would work and that sometimes new ideas don't work right away. If the child is still having problems at the end of the test period, another plan can be brainstormed when you meet.

It is the child's responsibility to keep the evaluation appointment. If the child forgets, don't remind the child; just let the time go by. Later, you could comment that the child did not bring up the problem at the agreed upon time, and you were wondering how things were going.

In the following situation, Judy, age 14, has a problem involving money. Her parents have been divorced for 5 years. Her father used to live in a nearby city, and Judy visited him every Christmas vacation. Now, her father has taken a job in a distant city. Although Judy lives with her mother, Sue, and has a good relationship with her, Judy still has a close relationship with her father and wants to continue the holiday visits. The total expense of the trip is beyond the combined financial resources of both her mother and father. Judy has an older sister in college and both parents contribute to expenses. Her parents have told Judy what they can afford, which amounts to about half the expenses.

Judy: I just don't know what I'm going to do, Mom. I can't earn enough by baby-sitting to get the rest of the money.

Sue: You sound very discouraged because earning the money seems impossible. (Step 1—perceive the problem)

Judy: Yeah. I mean, baby-sitting jobs are hard to get. Besides, they don't pay that much anyway. I guess I won't be going.

Sue: Seems as though you feel like giving up. (Step 1)

Judy: Uh huh. I don't see how I can do it.

Sue: Let's not give up yet. You said baby-sitting jobs are hard to get, and they don't pay that much. Do you want to talk about some other ways you might earn the money? (Step 2—propose ideas by asking Judy if she wants to discuss possibilities)

Judy: Yeah, I guess so. But I'm not old enough to work in a store.

Sue: That's right. But there must be other ways. What do some of your friends do? (Step 2)

Judy: Well, Carl mows lawns, but he's a boy so people will hire him to do that.

Sue: So you think people wouldn't hire a girl to do that? (Returning to Step 1)

Judy: I don't know.

Sue: How about making a list of all the possibilities, no matter how wild some may seem, and then we'll go over them. How does that sound to you? (Returning to Step 2)

Judy: That sounds all right.

Judy and her mother list all the ideas they can think of. Sue writes down all of Judy's ideas and mentions a couple of her own. In addition to baby-sitting and mowing lawns, they come up with delivering papers, washing neighborhood cars and windows, taking in laundry, and pet-sitting. They decide to post a list on neighbors' doors of the services she could provide.

Sue: OK. We've got a list of possibilities. Let's go through them one by one to see what you think. (Step 3—pick an idea)

They proceed through the list. Judy decides she would like to check out each idea to see how much time the task would involve and how much money she would make.

Sue: OK. You've agreed to check out each idea. How long
       do you think this will take? (Step 4—put the idea into
       action)

Judy: Maybe a couple of weeks.

Sue: Shall we talk it over again in 2 weeks to see what
       you've come up with? (Step 5—plan a time for evalua-
       tion)

Judy: OK.

Sue: Tell you what, I'll check with my friends and at work
       to see who needs what services if you want me to.
       (Returning to Step 2)

Sue understands and respects Judy's feelings about her father.
While Judy owns this problem, Sue is willing to help her figure
out how she's going to earn the money. Notice Sue did not tell
Judy what to do or how to do it. Instead, she stimulated Judy's
thinking and encouraged her.

Exploring Alternatives for Parent-Owned Problems

When you have a problem with your child and requests and
I-messages fail, it may be time to negotiate. Exploring alternatives is very useful in negotiating conflicts. The same steps out-
lined in solving child-owned problems are used in negotiation,
with some slight differences in their application.

1. *Perceive the Problem.* This step is used to clarify feelings,
beliefs, and facts from both your and the child's side of the issue:
One way to begin the discussion is with an I-message. "Scott, I
have something I want to talk with you about. When _____, I
feel _____ because _____." The I-message states the problem as you see it. Often, the child will respond with his own
form of an I-message. Be prepared to switch to reflective listening. Use open-ended questions if necessary. In the following
example, Scott has forgotten to feed the cat as he agreed to do
and his father, Milt, is explaining how he feels.

Milt: When Igore is not fed, I get concerned because he
       cries, and I know how uncomfortable hunger can be.
       (I-message)

Scott: (angrily) I forget a couple of times and you come unglued!

Milt: You're very angry and think I'm nagging you. It's not my intention to nag, but I'm concerned about Igore. How can we work this out so you remember? (Switching to reflective listening and an open-ended question)

Keep an open mind and assure the child you want to reach a resolution to the problem that will be acceptable to both of you. Make sure you choose a time when there is no conflict to talk to the child. Keep calm and focus on the issue.

2. *Propose Ideas.* Even though this is your problem, it's best to get the child's ideas first. He'll feel more cooperative if he comes up with ideas. Add yours only if needed. If children feel respected and appreciated, they'll often be willing to help you out. Encourage creativity through brainstorming.

3. *Pick an Idea.* The idea chosen must be acceptable to both of you. Together, evaluate each proposed idea. Ask if the idea is acceptable to the child and then state your own opinion. Discard ideas that are not acceptable to both of you.

4. *Put the Idea into Action.* Once an idea or combination of ideas has been chosen, it's time for a commitment. Make sure the chosen idea is one you are both willing to live with. Trying to force the child to accept an idea or trying to live with one that is uncomfortable for you won't solve the problem.

Ask the child if he is willing to experiment with the idea and state what you are willing to do. Sometimes it is necessary to build in consequences for each of you if the agreement is broken. You could say, "If either one of us breaks this agreement, what will be the consequences?" Decide on a consequence for you and then discuss consequences for the child. You may need to return to brainstorming to establish consequences.

Salvador's two boys have agreed to clean up the kitchen after dinner before watching TV, and Salvador has agreed not to nag them about the chore. To help everyone stick to the agreement, Salvador and his children have decided on consequences for breaking the agreement. If the boys forget to clean the kitchen and begin to watch TV, Salvador will simply shut off the set without saying a word (to avoid giving them undue attention for forgetting). The TV can be turned on after the kitchen is clean. If Salvador nags, then the deal is off, and the kitchen is his responsibility.

Consequences, unlike most punishments, are logically related to the misbehavior, often set up and agreed on in advance, and don't involve threats and reminders. (The concept of consequences is discussed more fully in Chapter 7.)

5. *Plan a Time for Evaluation.* Decide how long the agreement will be in effect and set a time to discuss the results of the agreement. Since this is your problem, you take the responsibility for making sure the follow-up meeting takes place.

The following example shows how negotiation with children about a parent-owned problem can work. Bob and Nadia each have custody of their children. Bob is concerned about his relationship with his stepson, Dmitri, age 8.

Bob:	Dmitri, it seems you've been pretty angry with me lately. I'd really like to find out why and see if we can get along better. Will you tell me what's wrong? (Step 1—perceive the problem)
Dmitri:	I don't know.
Bob:	Well, earlier today, you yelled at me when I asked you to take out the trash. When I'm yelled at, I get concerned because something's wrong. (Step 1)
Dmitri:	You treat your kids better than me!
Bob:	So, you're angry because you think I'm unfair? (Step 1)
Dmitri:	Yeah. You're always trying to make me do things and they don't do nothing!
Bob:	You think Joy and Joe don't do their share. (Step 1)
Dmitri:	Yeah, that's right!
Bob:	OK. What can we do about this? (Step 2—propose ideas)
Dmitri:	Make them do things.
Bob:	Shall we discuss who does what at our family meeting this week? (Step 3—pick an idea)

Dmitri: Yeah.

Bob: Is there anything else you're angry about? (Returning to Step 1)

Dmitri: Well, when my dad lived here, he used to take me places—just me and him.

Bob: So you would like for just you and me to go some places together? (Step 1)

Dmitri: Yeah.

Bob: Well, I'd like to do that too. Would it also be fair for Joy and Joe and me to go some places by ourselves too? (Step 1)

Dmitri: Yeah, I guess so.

Bob: OK. Let's talk about some places we could go. (Step 2)

Bob and Dmitri discussed several options: ball games, movies, and the video arcade (Step 2). They decided on a local high school football game for their first outing (Step 3 and Step 4—put the idea into action). They agreed to talk about how it went and plan another activity after the game (Step 5—plan a time for evaluation).

In this discussion, Bob was very patient with Dmitri. He reflected Dmitri's feelings several times and stated his own. Dmitri was longing for adult male companionship—something he missed since his dad had moved to another town. Bob made it clear that he would be spending time with all the family's children. Dmitri seemed to understand this.

Sometimes, no matter how much effort you put into it, you and the child don't reach agreement. If your negotiation session isn't effective you can:

- Return to brainstorming.
- Table the issue to give both of you an opportunity to think about the problem.
- Make the decision yourself if the problem must be resolved. Be careful about doing this. Examine the situation to see if you can live with indecision for a while. If not, inform the child that since agreement has not been reached, you'll have to make a temporary decision. Plan a

time to talk again and assure the child you are willing to listen and consider any other suggestion he has at that time.

The Family Meeting

So far this chapter has discussed how to hold individual problem-solving sessions with children. Now you will see how to get the whole family involved in decision making.

The family meeting is a forum for making family decisions. Holding family meetings in single-parent families and stepfamilies is essential. If you are a single parent, you are probably the only adult in the household. You need the cooperation of your children to make the household run smoothly. Stepfamily parents and children bring different customs and values to the new family. Learning to compromise is often the backbone of success in stepfamilies. Differences can be discussed, agreements can be made, and new traditions can be established in family meetings.

Many families have meetings but few have family meetings. A family meeting is an orderly, regularly scheduled activity. Meetings held on the spot to handle a crisis often fail due to the atmosphere of the meetings and the irregular nature of them. In fact, waiting until a crisis occurs before discussing feelings and issues can be very damaging to relationships.

When a family meeting is a regularly scheduled event that family members can count on, each person knows he will have the opportunity to be involved in family decisions. In most families, meeting once a week is sufficient.

While problems are solved in family meetings, holding family meetings strictly to solve problems produces a negative tone, dissatisfaction, and disinterest. Nobody wants to meet regularly just to solve problems. Family meetings are opportunities for the family to work together and enjoy each other. Such meetings give each member the opportunity to:

- Share feelings, beliefs, and opinions and be listened to
- Give encouragement and positive feedback to each other

- Settle disagreements
- Distribute family responsibilities
- Plan family fun

Starting Family Meetings

There are several ways to begin family meetings. The method chosen depends on what you believe will be effective in your family. Some parents find simply explaining the purpose of family meetings and starting with a formal agenda works best. The following is a sample agenda.

1. Share the good things that happened in the family since the last meeting.

2. Give "appreciation strokes"—that is, have members tell what they appreciate about each other. You can model this by using positive I-messages to tell what contributions you appreciate from each family member. "When you _____, I appreciated it because _____."

3. Discuss the minutes from the last meeting.

4. Review and discuss old business.

5. Discuss new business. Be sure that you include planning family fun.

6. Summarize agreements.

7. Evaluate how the family thinks the meeting went and the decisions that were made.

Other parents find the "back-door" approach more appropriate to starting family meetings in their family. They begin by having informal meetings around the dinner table and discussing issues on which they are sure agreement will be reached, such as family fun. "Heavier" issues, such as problems and distribution of chores, are gradually worked into the informal meetings. Eventually, after the family is working together, the parents introduce formal family meetings.

Some parents find polling individual members about the idea of having family meetings works best in their situation. They get everyone's opinion and begin with those members who are willing to attend.

Effective Family Meeting Guidelines

Establishing family meetings is one of the most challenging tasks discussed in this program. It's one thing to deal with children on a one-to-one basis and quite another to deal with the family as a group. Yet effective family meetings are required for a functioning democratic family. It's difficult, if not impossible, to gain lasting cooperation without them. Effective family meetings don't just happen. They require effort, commitment, and following certain guidelines.

Share the meeting responsibilities. The first few meetings are chaired by the parent or parents to provide a model of leadership and structure. Then the leadership is rotated in whatever way the family chooses. Taking minutes of the family meeting is another responsibility to be rotated. Parents and older siblings can help young children with taking the minutes, perhaps by helping the children summarize the minutes on a tape recorder.

Start and end the meeting on time. Meetings without established time limits violate respect for everyone's time and produce limited cooperation. Decide together when meetings will start and when they will end. Stick to the time limits.

Meetings with young children may be 15 or 20 minutes long. Teenagers can handle meetings of 45 minutes to an hour. In households with children of different ages, 30 minutes may be an effective time compromise. You know your family and what they will sit still for.

Decide on ground rules. Ground rules that all family members understand and accept help meetings run more smoothly. Brainstorm the rules at your first formal meeting. If the family has difficulty, you could present the following rules, saying you've heard some families operate with these rules. Get everyone's reactions to them.

1. Stick to the topic.
2. Listen to each other.
3. Encourage each other.
4. Give everyone a chance to talk.
5. Make decisions together.

Make a rules poster and display it so that everyone can see the rules each time you meet. Younger children may wish to draw pictures to illustrate each rule. This can also help young children who have limited reading skills remember the rules.

Make decisions together. Use the exploring alternatives process to make plans and decisions and to make sure everyone understands the problem or situation being discussed. Get the feelings and the facts and clarify beliefs and opinions. Once the problem or issue is understood, the family should propose ideas. Encourage participation in the discussion and decision making. Get the children's ideas first, adding yours if necessary. If a child isn't participating, ask the child directly for an opinion or idea.

Next have the family evaluate each idea and pick one that is agreeable to everyone. Although in political democracies decisions are made by majority rule, this is not appropriate in family meetings. Voting produces resentment on the part of the losers.

Work for consensus, in which everyone agrees on an idea. If the family fails to reach consensus on the issue:

- Table it to give everyone a chance to think.
- Make a temporary decision yourself if the issue must be settled. Use this approach infrequently and only when necessary.

The family puts what they have decided on into action by making a commitment to keeping the agreement. This may also involve deciding who will take on what responsibilities to see the plan is carried out. Agreements are in effect until the next meeting. They are then evaluated under old business. If someone complains between meetings, parents can reply, "We agreed to do this until the next family meeting. Bring up your complaints then." The family may need to discuss consequences (see Chapter 7) for broken agreements. This is especially the case when forgotten chores are involved.

The family's first decisions are when and where to hold meetings. The time chosen must be a time when everyone can attend. The meeting place needs to be comfortable and arranged so all members can see each other. If your family decides to hold meetings around the dinner table, hold the meeting after the meal when the dishes are cleared.

Issues That Can Be Decided at Family Meetings

Almost any issue facing the family is appropriate for discussion in the family meeting. But because you have family meetings does not mean you give the control of the family to the children; it does mean you share control with them. You may consider certain issues inappropriate for family decision making, such as accepting a promotion that will require different family routines. But the more decisions the family can make together, the more opportunities for cooperation. Here is a list of some typical issues many parents discuss in family meetings. See if you can add to the list for your family.

- Family outings
- Vacations
- Plans for stepsibling visits

- Plans for company
- Distribution of chores
- Allowances
- Conduct of friends in house
- Differences in family values
- Family finances

- Family rules
- Bedtimes
- Use of family property (telephone, TV, car)
- Mealtimes and menus

_____

_____

_____

In addition to making plans and decisions, solving problems, and giving encouragement, family meetings also serve as forums for giving information and sharing feelings on decisions not made in the family meeting. For example, if a parent is transferred to another city by her company, she may not feel her decision on whether to go should be made by the family, but the family members do need an opportunity to share their feelings about the move.

Everyone in the family needs the opportunity to bring up issues for discussion. If the parents dominate what is discussed, the children will soon lose interest. Many families establish an agenda book in which family members can sign up to bring issues to the family meeting. Issues are discussed at the meeting in the order recorded in the book. Parents or older siblings can help young children put down anything they want to discuss. If there are other issues that aren't recorded, they must wait until the recorded issues are discussed.

Family Meeting Leadership Skills

Good group leadership skills are required for effective family meetings. The following skills will help your meetings run smoothly. Modeling these skills will also help your children to learn them.

Structuring. Structuring simply refers to keeping the meeting on task. The leader may structure the meeting by bringing up topics for discussion, keeping the discussion on the topic, and helping the family follow the guidelines for effective meetings. If the discussion wanders off the topic, all the leader needs

to say is "I think we're getting off the topic. We were discussing
_____. Would you like to say something about that topic?"

Universalizing. By observing and pointing out similar feelings and opinions of family members, the meeting leader univer-
salizes to help members identify when they share a concern.
Simple questions and statements, such as "Does anyone else feel
like Carla does?" or "Ted, you and Vicki seem to have the same
opinion about this," help members become aware of any similar
thoughts and feelings.

Redirecting. It is important for the meeting leader to
encourage and promote interaction and discussion between all
family members at the meeting. The leader can call for members'
ideas by saying something like, "Does anyone have a comment
on that?" or "Katherine, what is your opinion?" Or, if members
direct their communication only toward the meeting leader, the
leader can redirect comments by saying, "Tell your idea to the
group."

Redirecting encourages brainstorming. When the family
brainstorms, holding evaluation of ideas until all are given, creativity is encouraged.

Promoting direct interaction. Sometimes members will
attempt to make comments about each other's ideas through
the leader. When this happens, the leader encourages members
to speak directly to each other. If the leader consistently
responds to indirect communication by simply stating, "Please
speak directly to _____," family members will soon catch on.

Summarizing. Summaries are appropriate after a long discussion or when there are different opinions. The end of the
meeting also calls for a summary.

Giving feedback. Giving feedback involves reflective listening. When someone shares a feeling message, feed back the
feelings and facts you hear. Giving feedback also involves
respectfully telling family members what you think of their
behavior or beliefs. Remember feedback is not limited to problems. It can be used for encouragement also.

Sometimes one family member will do or say something that
disrupts the meeting or is disrespectful to another member.
When this happens, the leader can give feedback and encourage
others to give feedback through I-messages directed to the

offending member: "Jayson, how did you feel when Kent said that to you? Tell Kent how you feel."

Giving encouragement. If family meetings are to be effective, an encouraging atmosphere must prevail. Offer encouragement to members by showing appreciation. Ask them to encourage each other by focusing on each other's efforts and contributions.

Dealing with Family Members Who Won't Attend Meetings
In some families, certain members are enthusiastic about family meetings and others are resistant. Those who are resistant may believe the meetings won't be effective or that they stand a chance of losing some power.

It does no good to try to force resistant members to attend meetings—their resistance is just increased. The most effective thing to do is to meet with family members who are ready. As the willing members make plans and decisions, these agreements will affect nonattending members. Reluctant members usually decide it's more beneficial for them to attend meetings so they have their say in decisions that affect them.

> Sally has custody of her three children: Jack, age 15, Mitzi, age 13, and Steve, age 12. When Sally introduced the idea of holding family meetings, Mitzi and Steve were interested, but Jack thought the idea would be a waste of time and refused to attend. At their first meeting, Sally told Mitzi and Steve that she had some changes in her job that would require her to bring work home from the office. She asked for their help with the chores she usually did for the family. Mitzi and Steve volunteered to take over doing the laundry. They decided to set up a hamper where dirty clothes would be placed. What was in the hamper by Saturday would be washed.
>
> Jack played on a local baseball team and was required to have a clean uniform for each game. One Monday afternoon before a game, Jack asked his mom where his clean uniform was. Sally told him of the agreement made at the family meeting. Jack said, "But I wasn't told about this!" and Sally replied, "I'm sorry you weren't at the meeting when this was decided." When Jack said, "Well, what do I do now?" Sally shrugged her shoulders and politely replied, "I don't know, Jack." Jack sat on the bench during the game and came to the next family meeting.

"Boy! Next time I'm going to the family meeting!"

It's important to avoid making decisions that affect nonattending members as a way of forcing their participation. This will be met with increased resistance. Simply make the decisions that are necessary to improve family functioning and let the nonattending members experience the results of the decisions.

Holding Family Meetings with Young Children

Even infants can participate in family meetings just by being there. Holding an infant or setting a toddler in a high chair during the meetings helps the child get used to the meeting as a regular family occurrence. As they mature and can communicate effectively, the children's participation becomes active and useful. Invite their feelings and ideas. Show appreciation for their contributions. Their attention spans may be short and they may wander in and out of the meetings. This is OK as long as they aren't disturbing the meeting.

The more young children become involved in family meetings, the more their skills of decision making and group participation develop. As a child reaches school age, she can learn to lead family meetings with the parent's or older sibling's help.

Family Meetings in Single-Parent Families

Family meetings involve all members in a particular household. In single-parent families, there is usually only one adult present in the household. In some ways, this makes the family meeting simpler; the parent can set the tone by herself. Single parents need family meetings to gain the cooperation of the children in running a household with limited adult availability. Children in single-parent homes have increased responsibilities, and they can learn to accept these responsibilities and gain a feeling of importance in making the family function through family meetings.

The following example of a portion of a family meeting in a single-parent family involves George and his two children—Tony, age 9, and Tina, age 7. Until recently, George has had a sitter available from the time the children returned from school until he got home from work. Since his sitter has moved and another is not readily available, George has to figure out how to provide for his children while he's at work. The local day-care center is filled, so George has to help his children learn how to take care of themselves at home until he gets home from work. He discusses the situation with his children in a family meeting. Notice the steps of exploring alternatives and the group leadership skills he uses.

George: We need to talk about how you will take care of yourselves after school until I get home. First, let's talk about the house key. (Structuring) What are some ways you can make sure you have a key available? Let's think of all the ideas we can and then we'll decide which one will work the best. Who has an idea? (Step 1—perceive the problem and Step 2—propose ideas)

Tony: I could just keep a key in my pocket.

George: OK. That's an idea. Tina, what's your idea? (Step 2 and redirecting)

Tina: You could leave a key at Mrs. Walter's, and we could pick it up from her.

George: OK. Any other ideas? No? Let's discuss these ideas. (Step 3—pick an idea and structuring) What do you think of Tony's idea of keeping the key in his pocket? (Step 3 and redirecting)

Tina: He might lose it.

Tony: I would not!

George: Tony, it seems you're insulted by Tina's comment. I don't think it's an insult. Losing the key concerns me too. (Step 1 and giving feedback and universalizing) Anybody can lose a key. (Step 1 and giving encouragement by making key loss a common possibility) How about wearing it around your neck on a chain? (Step 2 and redirecting)

Tony: That's baby stuff!

George: Let's skip ahead to the next idea for now. (Step 3 and structuring) What about leaving it at Mrs. Walter's? (Step 3 and redirecting)

Tony: Well, what if she's not home some day?

George: Good point. (Giving encouragement) Tina, you and I are concerned Tony might accidentally lose the key and he doesn't want to wear it on a chain around his neck. (Step 1 and summarizing) Have you got an idea how he could make sure the key's not lost? (Step 2 and redirecting)

Tina: No.

George: Tony, how else could you keep the key so we'll feel good about it? (Step 2 and redirecting)

Tony: Well, maybe I could get one of those key ring things that hooks on to my belt.

George: Tina, what do you think about that? Is that OK with you? (Step 3 and redirecting)

Tina: Yeah.

George: Me too. OK. We'll do that. (Step 4—put the idea into action) Now, let's talk about what you do when you get home. How can you make sure you are safe when you get home? (Step 3 and structuring and redirecting)

Notice that George moved back and forth between Steps 1, 2, and 3 of exploring alternatives as they were needed. The evaluation of the plan would occur in the next family meeting. George effectively used appropriate leadership skills to make the meeting go smoothly.

Family Meetings in Stepfamilies

Blending two sets of customs and values is a challenging task of stepfamily living. The family meeting is a valuable resource for achieving this task. Each family member needs to realize that no one member's particular ways are better than another's; they are just different. Whether the toothpaste tube is squeezed in the middle or at the end is not the real issue. The "squeeze" becomes the conflict. As the family decides together, differences can be resolved and agreements and compromises can be made.

Even when children are only with you part time, they still need to be included in the family meeting. It gives them more information and helps them feel valued. Meeting with all family members encourages the family to function together as a cooperative unit.

The following example of part of a family meeting in a stepfamily involves Alex and Nancy and their children. Mary, age 14, is Alex's child and John and Ann, ages 13 and 10, are Nancy's children. The family has been holding family meetings for a few weeks. In the following excerpt, John is the leader.

John: OK. That's settled. Mary, you're next on the agenda. It says on the list, "family eating together at dinner." What does this mean? (Step 1—perceive the problem and structuring and redirecting)

Mary: Well, when Dad and I lived alone, we always had dinner together at the table. Now everyone just grabs their food and eats in front of the TV.

John: You don't like that, then. (Step 1 and giving feedback)

Mary: Yeah. Well, you know, it's all right, but Dad and I used to talk over dinner, and that was really neat.

Nancy: You miss that time with Dad. (Step 1 and giving feedback)

Mary: Yeah.

John: Has anybody got any ideas about how to handle this problem? (Step 2 and redirecting)

Ann: Why don't Mary and Alex go ahead and have their dinner at the table, and we'll . . . .

John: (Politely interrupting) Ann, please tell Mary and Alex your idea. (Step 2 and promoting direct interaction)

Ann: Oh, yeah. I forgot. Mary, why don't you and Alex have your dinner at the table, and we'll eat by the TV like we always do?

Nancy: Well, I think everyone should eat together.

John: OK. You don't like that idea. (Giving feedback)

Alex: John, let's brainstorm. You know, get everyone's ideas and not talk about them until we're done—even if we don't like some of them. (Step 2—propose ideas and structuring)

John: Oh, yeah. OK. For now let's write down that idea. (Structuring) Who else has got an idea? (Step 2 and redirecting)

Mary: We could trade nights. You know, one night we eat at the table and the next night we eat in front of the TV.

Ann: But what if there's a good show on the night we're supposed to eat at the table?

John: Ann, remember we're just brainstorming now. (Step 2 and structuring) So, let's put that idea down. I have an idea. Maybe we could check the TV news each week and decide what it is we want to watch as a family. (Step 2)

Ann: I like that idea.

Mary: Yeah, me too.

Alex: I'll go along with that.

Nancy: That's OK with me. It looks like we all agree on this idea. (Step 3—pick an idea)

John: OK. I guess it's settled. Are we going to experiment with it this week to see how it works? (Step 4—put the idea into action, Step 5—plan a time for evaluation and structuring)

The family looked at the TV schedule for the week and decided there were four shows they wanted to watch. On the other nights, they would eat together at the table.

Several leadership skills were used in the meeting. While there were no specific encouraging statements, the atmosphere John and the parents set was an encouraging atmosphere.

This dialogue illustrates how a stepfamily can work together to settle differences in family customs. As illustrated, sometimes an idea will be presented that has instant appeal and the approval of all the family members. When this happens, there's no need to continue.

Conflict Resolution Principles

Four conflict resolution principles can be used in individual negotiations and family meetings. The last three principles were developed by Dr. Rudolf Dreikurs.[1]

1. *Identify similarities.* Often in a conflict with another person you will be able to see the great differences in your values, beliefs, and attitudes. However, it is more helpful to examine closely the ways in which you may be similar to the person you disagree with on almost any issue. Is it possible that you are both showing and expressing love but from a different perspective? You may both believe that you are right. You may both believe that it is important to win or get your way. Are you similar in terms of your desire to have close friends or to be permitted to enjoy your particular interests? When you begin to look closely at the many ways in which you are similar to the person that you are in conflict with, it is interesting how you begin to have different perceptions of what appears to be their "selfish"

behavior. Sometimes you may see yourself reflected in the behavior of the person you are in conflict with: "Mick, I think that we both feel pride in our family, but we are expressing it in different ways. How could we work together to show our pride without you getting in trouble with your teacher and me getting mad at you?"

2. *Promote mutual respect.* As you have been learning throughout this book, mutual respect is important in all interactions between parents and children. When you are in conflict with someone, you can show respect for yourself and for the other person by avoiding fighting, giving in, and intimidation. In a group meeting when everyone is arguing and talking at once, you can say (in a friendly way) something like, "When everyone talks at once, it is very distracting and disrespectful to each other. Let's listen and respect each other's feelings."

3. *Discuss the real issues.* Sometimes in a disagreement, the real issue is not the one on which people seem to be disagreeing. The real issue will often involve winning, showing power, proving who is right, or other individual goals and values. When these issues get in the way of solving the problem, they need to be addressed: "It seems everyone thinks his way is the right way. How will trying to prove who is right help us solve this problem?"

4. *Change the current agreement.* When you are in conflict with someone you have an agreement that you may not be aware of; you are agreeing to argue or to fight. In order to cooperate and reach a new agreement, you will have to decide what you are willing to do to change the agreement, not tell others what they should do. For example, you might say, "Looks like we've decided to argue about how to distribute the chores rather than working out a cooperative agreement. I'm willing to continue discussing this issue if others are willing to work toward a solution we can all accept." If the others are willing to create a mutual agreement, brainstorm ideas to find an idea everyone is willing to live with. The following chart summarizes the conflict resolution principles for you.

◆ ◆ ◆

Chart 6. Conflict Resolution Principles

Principle	*Explanation*
Identify similarities.	Examine closely the ways in which you may be similar to the person you disagree with. Do you have similar values, emotions, or desires?
*Promote mutual respect.	Show respect for yourself and the other person by avoiding fighting, giving in, and intimidation. Listen to and respect each other's feelings.
Discuss the real issues.	Talk about the individual goals and values that are often the real issues in an argument and that get in the way of solving the problem.
Change the current agreement.	Become aware of your agreement to argue and fight. Cooperate to reach a new agreement. Brainstorm ideas to find a solution everyone is willing to accept.

*The last three principles were developed by Rudolph Dreikurs.

Exploring alternatives with children and holding family meetings are certainly not cure-alls for every family ill, but they do provide the opportunity for maximum cooperation. The "family that decides together, resides together" in the sense that they have a commitment to family strength and harmony. If you will give full effort to exploring alternatives and making family meetings work, you'll find the stresses of daily family living decreasing. The system of discipline presented next depends in part upon exploring alternatives and family decision making.

Activity Assignment

During the next week, practice exploring alternatives and hold a family meeting.

Important Points to Remember in Chapter 6

1. Exploring alternatives is a process that can be used to help children resolve problems, negotiate parent-child and family conflicts, and make decisions in the family meeting.

2. Exploring alternatives involves the five *P's* of problem solving.

- Perceive the problem.
- Propose ideas.
- Pick an idea.
- Put the idea into action.
- Plan a time for evaluation.

3. When a child owns a problem, the parent helps the child explore alternative ways to solve it. The parent uses reflective listening and open-ended questions to perceive the problem and then helps the child seek his own solutions through brainstorming. The child decides on an idea and makes a commitment to experiment with the plan for a certain length of time. A follow-up meeting is held to examine the results of the plan.

4. When the parent owns a problem, the parent explores alternatives with the child to reach a mutually acceptable solution. Sometimes it's necessary to build in consequences for both the parent and child in case the agreement is broken. The solution is put into action for an agreed upon length of time and then evaluated.

5. The family meeting is a regularly scheduled event that serves as a forum for family decision making. Family meetings give each member opportunities to:

- Share feelings, beliefs, and opinions and be listened to
- Give encouragement and positive feedback
- Settle disagreements
- Distribute family responsibilities
- Plan family fun

6. Family meetings can be begun with a formal agenda or more informally as discussions of family fun.

7. Guidelines for effective family meetings include:

- Share the meeting responsibilities
- Start and end the meeting on time
- Decide on ground rules
- Make decisions together

8. Everyone in the family needs the opportunity to bring up issues for discussion. Almost any issue facing the family is appropriate for discussion in a family meeting.

9. Family meeting leadership skills include:

- Structuring
- Universalizing
- Redirecting
- Promoting direct interaction
- Summarizing
- Giving feedback
- Giving encouragement

10. Begin family meetings with those who are willing to attend. Nonattending members are subject to agreements of the meeting.

11. Infants and young children can be involved in the family meetings as long as they don't disturb the meetings.

12. Family meetings are important in single-parent families because they help the parent gain the cooperation of the children and help children accept their increased responsibilities.

13. Family meetings in stepfamilies are valuable in blending the two sets of family customs and values.

14. Four conflict resolution principles can be used in individual negotiations and family meetings:

- Identify similarities
- Promote mutual respect
- Discuss the real issues
- Change the current agreement

Chapter 7

Discipline

Discipline is a major concern for parents. Single parents find they are totally responsible for discipline when they are with their children. Parents in stepfamilies find they may bring very different styles of discipline to the new family. The challenge of respecting each other's style and trying to blend styles can be a problem. Also, both single parents and stepparents may be very critical of an ex-spouse's style of discipline.

Discipline is often thought of as a synonym for punishment. But punishment is only one form of discipline, and an ineffective one at that. Punishment is the primary type of discipline that was used when our society was more autocratic and less democratic. In an autocratic society, people function on the basis of superiors and inferiors. The husband is considered the final word on all decisions in the family, the wife is in a secondary position, and the children are considered to be inferior to both of the parents. Many parents were raised in a controlled, demanding, autocratic society that appeared effective but did not establish cooperative relationships. Within an autocratic structure, things may work reasonably well on the surface. However, a lot of anger, hostility, and resistance exists below the surface.

Our society has changed toward more equality and respect for all of its members. The labor movement, the civil rights movement, and the women's liberation movement have helped bring about this change.

The tradition of controlling children through punishment and reward, in addition to promoting inequality, is just not effective. Children rebel and get even when punished and tend to consider rewards as their right. Some people see permissiveness as an alternative to punishment and reward. They may be guided by memories of childhood punishment and restriction. Permissive parents attempt to avoid conflict by giving in and essentially turning over the child's rearing to the child. These parents feel powerless, and they act almost as if they are trying to win their children's acceptance. Permissiveness cannot work because it removes respect from both the child and the parent. When children are treated as beyond control and the parents behave as if they have no way of restoring order, there is little opportunity for the relationship to be an effective one.

Effective Parent-Child Relationships

The word *discipline* in this book means "training that develops self-control, character, or orderliness and efficiency" and disciplined behavior is "self-control or orderly conduct."[1] Further, discipline is viewed as a learning process.

The discipline system presented in this book is one of the most effective systems in a society striving for social equality. It is based on equality and mutual respect, provides choices within limits, and requires acceptance of responsibility for the consequences of one's choices. This system is called *democratic discipline*. Democratic discipline is not permissive; there are limits in a democracy, but there are choices within those limits.

Equality and mutual respect are the basis of effective parenting relationships and of effective discipline. Effective parent-child relationships include the following attitudes and characteristics.

1. Mutual respect and mutual trust
2. Mutual involvement, concerns, and caring about the relationship
3. Understanding of each other's feelings
4. Willingness to hear each other and to communicate honestly and openly
5. Focus on what is positive and good about the relationship rather than an emphasis on mistakes and weaknesses
6. Commitment to work at resolving conflicts

7. Common goals for the family and independent goals for the individuals

8. Acceptance of each other as imperfect, caring, concerned, and interested in improving the relationship

The development of mutual respect between all family members is a necessary component for making the new family unit thrive. All families—regardless of structure—need this to enable the family to grow.

When family members learn to live together as equals, they have no need to exert their superiority, punish or control each other, or show their power by putting others down. When a democratic relationship exists in the family: " . . . respect replaces rebellion, and cooperation replaces coercion."[2] Single parents and stepfamily parents will find mutual respect can provide the encouragement needed to survive the rough spots in building a new family and help the family grow stronger each day.

Prevention of Discipline Problems

There are two sides to the discipline coin: prevention of problems and correction of them. Obviously the more problems you prevent, the fewer you have to correct.

Problems can be prevented by giving children control of their own lives in areas that they are ready to handle. Obviously you wouldn't let your 3-year-old child decide whether or not to run in the street. But you could give him a choice of playing in the yard or playing inside the house. If he decided to play out in the street, you could assume he's decided to play inside the house since the limit you set for his playing outside was to stay in the yard.

Children, like adults, don't like to be controlled by someone else. So, the more you can put them in charge of their own lives, the more cooperation you can gain. Think of the areas your children could be responsible for—either through individual choice or through participating in family decisions in the family meeting. Here are some ideas. See if you can add to the list.

- Chores
- How to spend their allowance
- Clothing (considering budget and types needed)
- Menu planning
- Vacations
- Family outings
- Homework
- Routines
- Family customs and rules

- Hobbies and activities
- Friends
- Bedtimes
- Toys (within budget)
- How to keep their rooms
- Whether or not to accompany parents on outings

_____

_____

_____

Correcting Problems with Natural and Logical Consequences

Consider the consequences of reward and punishment. When parents reward or punish children, they take responsibility for the children's behavior. They don't allow the children to develop self-discipline. Children often rebel against punishment and refuse to do anything unless rewarded. Children also get even with parents for punishing them, and some children will not respond to any reward. Furthermore, punishment is based on fear and submission, and rewards teach children to expect payment for the slightest contribution. Is this what you want to teach your children?

Doing away with reward and punishment without replacing the system would create chaos. An effective alternative to reward and punishment is a system of natural and logical consequences.

Natural and logical consequences permit children to choose their behavior within limits and be accountable for their choices.[3] A natural consequence involves the results of violating the law of nature. For example, if you go to bed late and have to get up early, you will be tired. If you go without lunch, you probably will be hungry before dinner. Natural consequences require no interference from the parent. The parent just stands by and lets the child learn through experiencing the consequences.

Many misbehaviors are not governed by natural consequences and some natural consequences are dangerous. In these cases, logical consequences are applied. A logical consequence involves the results of violating the rules of cooperation. If we are to live together, each person must be responsible for his own behavior and cooperate with others. Parents design logical consequences, often with the help of the child, especially with older children. To be a logical consequence, the result must fit the misbehavior. For example, if you don't pay your phone bill, you will experience the logical consequence of having your phone service disconnected.

Natural Consequences
The following are examples of situations in which natural consequences can be used.

Refusing to wear a coat. The child who refuses to wear a coat on a cold day becomes cold. Some parents object to using this natural consequence because they may have to put up with a cranky child if the child catches a cold. They fail to realize that there is no way to force a child to wear a coat. The child can always remove the coat when out of sight.

Refusing to eat what is served. A child who doesn't like what is served for dinner may refuse to eat. It's quite likely the child will be hungry later. But if you have established a rule that snacks are extras and only available if meals are eaten, the child will have to wait until breakfast to eat. That's OK. It's rare a child becomes ill from missing a meal.

Not going to bed on time. Children go through all sorts of maneuvers to avoid going to bed. Even when you force them into bed, you can't make them sleep. Why not let them learn on their own? Parents make too much fuss over sleep anyway. When children are not pressured, they will establish their own sleep requirements.

Bedtimes can be decided in a family meeting. At the agreed upon time, expect your children to be in their rooms. Young children can learn bedtimes by the "big hand, little hand" method of telling time or by the conclusion of certain activities. You can make bedtime pleasant for young children by reading them a story when the time comes.

If a child refuses to go to bed, don't get into a conflict with him. Withdraw your attention. Go to bed early, leaving him up, if necessary. Since his misbehavior isn't reinforced, the pleasures of staying up will most likely wear off. Refuse to be drawn into a power struggle. For example, if the child is noisy in an attempt to make you become involved, don't respond. If the child is determined, you may lose sleep for a few nights, but this is better than continual conflict at bedtime.

Logical Consequences

The following are examples of situations in which logical consequences can be used.

Allowances. Many parents are constantly handing out money for school lunches, movies, snacks, and so on. Some give allowances and then find they are still giving spending money as "loans" when the children run out of funds.

We believe children of school age can be taught to handle money through an allowance that covers most things— spending money and school lunches, for example. Then, if they spend it before the next allowance time, they have a problem. For example, not budgeting money may mean the child misses a lunch or two at school or a movie on the weekend. As children mature, a clothing allowance and money for savings can be included in the allowance.

Chores. As discussed in Chapter 6, the distribution of chores is best decided in the family meeting. Make the chore list together in the meeting. Include what you do to keep the household running so the children can see the full range of responsibilities. This reduces resentment when they are asked to choose chores.

Many families find establishing a "work-before-fun" rule solves getting chores done at agreed upon times. For example, if the

"We'll fill your plate when you fill Muffin's."

family has decided to clean the house on Saturday mornings, all family members, including the parents, must have their work done before turning to other things.

Some chores must be done on a daily basis. If the work-before-fun rule doesn't apply, the family can establish other priorities. The trash could be taken out or a pet could be fed before dinner, for example. If a child doesn't do the chore, nothing is said; he just isn't served dinner until the job is done. Individual checklists for chores, posted in a convenient place, can help children keep track of their progress and feel a sense of accomplishment.

Don't connect chores with allowances. This just invites conflict and teaches children to expect to be paid for everything they do for the family. Who pays you for what you do around the home for the family?

Designing Logical Consequences

Logical consequences and punishment are not the same, even though the action for a misbehavior may be similar in some cases. The manner and attitude in which the action is carried out make the difference. For example, suppose Loren, a teen-aged girl, is late from a date and her mother, Bev, "grounds" her. Bev is punishing Loren. The logical consequence of the teenager's being late could also be losing the privilege of going out the next time. But to use logical consequences, Bev and Loren must have made an agreement about what time Loren is to be home and what will happen if she is not home on time. If Loren is late, Bev will not say a word about Loren's breaking the agreement, but the next time Loren wants to go out, Bev will state the agreement and the fact that it was broken, which means Loren will have to stay home. Bev will also assure Loren of having another opportunity to demonstrate she'll keep the agreement: "You can go out next weekend if you're ready to keep the agreement."

Logical consequences are designed to fit the needs of a particular situation. Parents concentrate on controlling the situation instead of futile attempts to control the child.[4] For example, suppose you are trying to talk on the phone and your children are playing loudly in the room. What does this situation require? Obviously you need some quiet to hear what the person on the phone is trying to say. Instead of demanding the children "shut up," simply give them a choice that reflects the needs of the situation: "I'm sorry, but I can't hear. Either lower your voices or please go to another room to play." If they continue to make noise, they've chosen to leave the room.

The logic in logical consequences means the parental action fits the misbehavior. Some parents use withdrawal of privileges for every misbehavior. If a child swears, the parent takes away one TV program for every four-letter word. There's absolutely no logic in this approach—what does the TV have to do with swearing? The logical thing to do would be to take away attention from the child when she swears, leaving the room if necessary. Another possibility is to give the child a choice of not using those words in the parent's presence. If the child chooses to swear, she chooses to leave the room. Of course, the parent must be sure not to give the child a double standard by swearing himself.

Logical consequences deal with what will happen now and in the future. Punishment focuses on what happened in the past. For example, imagine your son wants to invite his friend Ed to stay overnight. The last time Ed came over, he and your son where noisy practically all night, and you didn't get much sleep trying to get them to be quiet. Instead of refusing to let Ed visit and reminding your son of the problem, set your limits: "Ed can stay over as long as both of you are willing to go to bed by _____ and be quiet so I can sleep." Then, if they make noise, you can take Ed home or deny another stay the next time your son asks because the agreement was broken.

Logical consequences are often set up in advance in a firm, but friendly, way. Punishment consists of threats. Advance consequences can involve a statement of your intentions, "If you come to the dinner table with unwashed hands, I'll assume you are not ready to eat," or agreements, "I'm sorry you spent your allowance and can't go to the movie with Jackie. But we agreed your allowance would cover those things, so I'm not going to lend you money." Consequences are delivered "on the spot" only if they involve disruptive behavior you can't ignore, the safety of the child or others, or the possibility of destruction of others' property: "Boys, I'm sorry but when you run in the house, you may break something. So, either stop running or go outside and run."

Mutual respect is vital to effective logical consequences. When parents punish, they violate respect for the child. When they give in, they violate respect for themselves. Your tone of voice, nonverbal behavior, and willingness to reject the act but not the child all show respect for the child. Your willingness to remain firm in holding to your limits maintains your respect for yourself.

> Patrick's daughter, Kelly, wants him to drive her to a school play. Patrick is busy with housework, so he tells her he will be happy to take her, but she'll need to help with some of his responsibilities so he is free to do the chauffeuring. They go over the list of chores and she picks taking Patrick's turn at washing the dishes after dinner before the two of them leave for the play. When it's time to leave for the play, the dinner dishes are still in the sink.

Kelly says, "Hey, Dad, let's go. We'll be late!" Patrick replies, "I'm sorry, Kelly, but the dishes are still in the sink. When the dishes are cleaned up, we can go." Kelly says anxiously, "But, Dad, we're late. I'll do them after I get back." Patrick calmly responds, "I'm sorry, but the agreement was to do them before we go." Patrick is friendly but also firm in his limits. He doesn't reject Kelly by lecturing or getting angry, but he expects her to keep her end of the bargain.

When parents use punishment, they demand obedience. When parents use consequences, they give choices and hold the child accountable. For example, if your child throws a temper tantrum, don't join her by demanding she calm down. Instead, leave the room if possible. Her choice, if she wants to be with you, is to quit screaming.

Punishment involves lectures, reminders, and nagging. When parents apply logical consequences, they simply give the child a choice and accept the child's decision. The child's behavior tells parents the decision. You can watch what your child does rather than listen to what the child says she will do. When applying a consequence you might comment on the behavior: "I see by your behavior you've decided . . ."

Once the consequence is chosen, the decision is irreversible at the time of the misbehavior. Don't give "chances" at that time. But, do assure the child he can have another opportunity to demonstrate he is ready to be cooperative in the near future. Tell the child when he may try again. On each repeat of the misbehavior, increase the time before the child can try again.

Do's and Don'ts for Using Consequences

There are certain actions that can make a consequence effective or ineffective. The following list will help you use consequences effectively.

1. *Let children experience consequences.* Many parents, perhaps because they feel sorry for their children, try to protect their children from consequences by punishing them or letting things go. Punishing places responsibility on the parent for the

behavior and letting things go teaches children they have a right to misbehave. This protection conveys lack of respect and confidence in the children's ability to be responsible for their behavior.

2. *Replace talk with action.* The first thing parents do when children misbehave is talk and reinforce the misbehavior. Children expect lectures. They don't expect silence. If the misbehavior needs immediate attention, restrict your words to what is necessary and present the consequence as a choice. Then act on your child's decision. For example, you could say to noisy children, "You can settle down or leave the room." If they don't settle down you could then say, "I see you've decided to leave the room."

3. *Phrase consequences respectfully.* Some ways to phrase consequences are: "You may _____ or _____. You decide." "You have a choice, either _____ or _____." You could also state your intentions and let the child decide: "I'm leaving at 7:00 if you want a ride." Or you could state the conditions of your involvement: "I'm willing to _____ if you are willing to _____." "You can if you're willing to _____."

4. *Put children all in the same boat.*[5] Parents pit children against each other if they try to seek out the culprit when the offender is unknown. The children end up in a "good guy, bad guy" game at each other's expense. Increasing competition and rivalry does not build family cooperation. If you return home and find, for example, that the bathroom mirror has been broken, don't hold an interrogation. Simply inform the children the mirror will need to be replaced. Don't listen to complaints; leave it up to them to figure out how the mirror will be replaced. Don't worry about being fair. Chances are the "good" children have had many opportunities to get their "bad" siblings in trouble before.

5. *Remain friendly as well as firm.* If your words, tone of voice, or nonverbal expressions contain any form of annoyance, anger, or hurt, your child will sense your negative feelings and these feelings will reinforce the misbehavior goal. Work on changing your expression of negative feelings. You can practice appropriate facial expressions in front of a mirror and listen to

your tone of voice on a tape recorder. If you rehearse being firm, but friendly, you'll find the negative feelings will vanish.

6. *Be consistent.* While no person can be totally consistent, you can increase your "batting average." Inconsistency reinforces children's misbehavior goals. If you respond one way when a child misbehaves and then change your response the next time the misbehavior occurs, the child will continue the misbehavior on the chance that she will receive the response she wants.

7. *Don't yield to others' opinions.* Don't cheat your children of learning to be responsible because your ex-spouse, grandparents, friends, or children's teachers may not like what you are doing. That's their problem. Which is more important, your children or other people's opinions of you? (More on responding to people who criticize your parenting style can be found in Chapter 8.)

8. *Don't dwell on the negative.* Children need to know they are OK. So, point out something positive soon after you confront the negative. Don't connect your positive comments with the misbehavior; this only calls attention to it. Instead, focus on something else such as a contribution to the family.

9. *Don't take on all problems at once.* Change is challenging for everyone. Take one problem at a time, starting where you feel you can be effective. Be aware that when you change your approach things often get worse before they get better.

10. *Don't create hidden intentions.* Logical consequences are effective if you allow the child to choose and accept the choice. Hidden intentions of "this will fix him," for example, will be sensed by the child and the consequence will fail. Remember that experience is the best teacher.

Dealing with Different Discipline Styles

Ideally, both parents in a family would have the same philosophy of child rearing. However, this is often not the case. Differences in child-rearing philosophies is one of the issues often leading to divorce. Stepfamily parents often bring differences in styles to the new family. But child-rearing conflicts, whether with your ex-spouse or your new partner, can be dealt with constructively.

The process of exploring alternatives is helpful in negotiating differences. By following the same steps you learned in Chapter 6 for dealing with children, you can negotiate the problem of differences in child-rearing styles.

It's best for you and your spouse or ex-spouse to develop a consistent style, if possible. But if you don't reach agreement, agree to disagree. Each of you will deal with the child in your own way (as long as child abuse is not involved, of course) on problems that each parent owns with the child. Resolve not to interfere with each other's dealings with the child as this only teaches the child to manipulate you. While it is better if parents have a similar approach, realize too that children have to learn to deal with all kinds of people with different relating styles. They are not fragile and they can handle it. When children move back and forth between households and are faced with different rules and expectations, they can choose how to respond in each situation.

Discipline Decisions for Single Parents and Stepparents

The following questions plague both single parents and stepparents.

1. Who is responsible for applying consequences?
2. How do I respond when children complain about how the other parent treats them?
3. How do I respond to children when they expect things from me the other parent permits that I don't agree with?

Deciding Who Applies Consequences

In single-parent homes where there's usually only one parent present, that parent is in complete charge of discipline when the children are with the parent. It's not appropriate for a parent to assume ownership of problems the other parent has with the children. This only causes confusion, interferes with the other parent's relationship with the child, and places an unnecessary burden on the interfering parent. The parent who is with the children is responsible for discipline when the children are in the parent's presence.

If you think your ex-spouse's methods are not teaching the children to become responsible and self-disciplined, you may decide to discuss the issue with your ex-spouse. Give your full effort to negotiating with your ex-spouse. If you can reach agreement, fine; if not, concentrate on your own relationship with the children when you are with them. One positive parent can counteract negative influences from the other parent.

Another question that concerns stepfamily parents is who applies consequences when the children are with the family, the biological parent or the stepparent? Stepparents often encounter resentment and resistance from their stepchildren if they immediately attempt to assume too much responsibility for disciplining. You can't effectively discipline children unless you have a positive relationship with them. Stepparents need to spend time developing a relationship before they put themselves in a disciplinary role.[6]

At times, biological parents will welcome someone to share the burden of childcare. But if biological parents turn the discipline over to the stepparents, they are asking for trouble in the new family. Turning the discipline over to the stepparent interferes with the relationship the stepparent needs to develop with the children.

When a stepparent assumes too much responsibility for discipline, the biological parent may resent what the stepparent is doing, even if he wanted to turn over the responsibility in the first place. The biological parent is then faced with the choice of confronting his spouse, which may create a breach in the marital relationship, letting the spouse deal with the children in discouraging ways, or undermining the spouse.

What is the best way to handle discipline in a stepfamily? Most families find the following guidelines offer the best alternative.

1. The parents discuss what they expect from each other.
2. The biological parent handles disciplinary problems, except those that occur between stepparent and stepchildren.[7]

3. The stepparent makes every effort to establish a relationship with the children through spending time with them and being encouraging. The stepparent disciplines only when the children do something that interferes with the stepparent's rights. For example, a stepparent may discipline if a stepchild borrows something from the stepparent and doesn't return it.

4. The biological parent gradually introduces the stepparent as one who is equally responsible for discipline by telling the children the stepparent is in charge in the biological parent's absence.[8]

5. As the relationships in the family grow, both parents will share the responsibility for discipline and work at developing a consistent style. If you and your spouse are studying these materials together, the two of you have an excellent opportunity to learn to use a democratic child-rearing style.

Handling Children's Complaints about Differences in Treatment

Children often complain about how another parent or stepparent treats them. Except in cases of child abuse, the children own their problems with others, including parents.

When a child complains, you can listen and, if necessary, use exploring alternatives to help the child deal with the issue. Of course, if you believe the other adult is being particularly discouraging to the child, you may decide to talk with the person. Do this without your child's knowledge, or you may give the impression that you will handle the child's problems with the other parent.

You may find that your children are difficult to deal with when they have been with their other parent or family. The other parent may permit behavior or privileges you don't permit. If the children compare life with the other parent to life with you and you come up short in their eyes, don't let them manipulate you. Refuse to become defensive or critical of the other parent. You can't decide what the other parent does, but you can decide how you respond to the children. For example, if your children complain they can do something when with the other parent that you don't permit when they are with you, simply acknowledge that you are sure they enjoy that activity, but that you don't agree with it nor will you permit the activity when they are with you. Stand firm in your limits and refrain from arguing. Change the subject or busy yourself with other activities.

Applying Your Skills for Effective Discipline

Effective discipline requires the establishment of a positive relationship between parents and children, based on mutual respect, caring, encouragement of self-esteem, and concern for each other's rights. Therefore, encouragement, reflective listening, I-messages, and exploring alternatives are just as much a part of an effective discipline system as natural and logical consequences. Encouragement underlies any effective approach with children. I-messages or consequences delivered without an encouraging attitude are nothing more than punishments in disguise.

When you are faced with a challenge in your parenting, you need to choose the skills that you have learned that will be the most effective. Some challenges are best met with a combination of reflective listening, I-messages, exploring alternatives, and logical consequences.

In their Thursday night family meeting, Stan and his family are discussing Stan's concern about family members leaving their possessions strewn around the house. Stan begins with an I-message: "When I see everyone's things left all around the house I feel let down because I work hard to keep the house clean for all of us, and I feel disrespected because everyone expects me to pick up the stuff." Reflective listening and more I-messages are used to gain understanding of everyone's feelings, beliefs, and opinions on the topic. Stan and his family explore alternatives and decide to place any items found out of place in the kitchen, living room, or bathroom in a holding box in the garage. They decide that the logical consequences for leaving one's possessions in public areas will be that the items are not returned for one day. Then the family member may have another opportunity to demonstrate he is ready to be responsible for the items. The atmosphere of the meeting is kept on an encouraging level so no member feels accused.

With some challenges, one or two approaches will apply. For example, if a child is complaining to you about too much homework, you can listen reflectively and help the child explore alternatives for organizing his time.

Logical consequences may be more effective than I-messages in some situations. For example, suppose you have an appointment and your 4-year-old, Debbie, is dawdling. Instead of telling her how you feel about the problem her dawdling is causing, you can simply give her a choice: "Debbie, we need to go now. You can choose to come to the car on your own or I can carry you. You decide."

Sometimes a logical consequence will follow an I-message if the message is ineffective. Be careful, though, not to make the consequence a punishment for not attending to your I-message. The consequence needs to be delivered simply as a natural follow-up to a problem that needs to be taken care of. For example, suppose your teenage son has just obtained his driver's license, and you are with him as a passenger. You are concerned that he's driving too fast and you send an I-message, which goes unheeded. You could then offer him the choice of slowing down or turning the driving over to you.

Consequences are more effective if they are negotiated through exploring alternatives, especially with older children and teenagers. When discussing a discipline problem, ask the child, "What do you think should happen if this continues?" If agreement is not reached, you can determine the consequence. Negotiation is not appropriate for minor issues (it makes them seem too important) nor does it apply to serious issues with limited choices, such as drinking or drug use. The skill or combination of skills you choose when faced with a parenting challenge depends on the following guidelines.

Consider the Child's Goal of Misbehavior

Sometimes certain approaches to solving problems with your child may reinforce the child's misbehavior goal. Reflective listening and exploring alternatives can reinforce the misbehavior goals of attention and power. I-messages can give undue attention, fuel power contests, and invite revenge, especially if used inappropriately—to overpower or get even. But, they can be effective in negotiation and family meetings when an atmosphere of mutual respect is established.

Natural consequences fit any goal because the parent doesn't have to interfere. Logical consequences, however, require participation by the parent. Logical consequences work best with attention getters because the behavior is usually minor. Power and revenge seekers may see logical consequences as punishment because they are in conflict situations with parents. It is best to take yourself out of the fight with a power or revenge seeker and discuss the problem later if needed. Use logical consequences only when behavior is disturbing and must be dealt with immediately. Do so by refusing to fight and simply giving the child a choice. Whenever possible, set up consequences in advance for anticipated misbehavior and follow through. Use encouragement and listening skills to build the relationship. The child who displays inadequacy is not disruptive, so logical consequences don't apply. Give this child lots of encouragement and use reflective listening and exploring alternatives.

Decide Who Owns the Problem

As you learned earlier, reflective listening is a skill that can be used when a child owns a problem and I-messages apply when you own a problem. Exploring alternatives can be used when you or the child owns the problem, depending on the situation.

Natural consequences apply to child-owned problems, such as a child's being cold because she doesn't wear a coat. Logical consequences can be used when the parent owns the problem. For example, if a parent comes to pick up a child for a visitation and the child is dawdling, the parent owns the problem. The parent can tell the child how long the parent will wait and let the child decide. If the parent leaves after the time has elapsed, chances are the child will be ready the next time. Sometimes logical consequences apply to problems children own. For example, if a child throws a tantrum to get candy in a store and her parent ignores her, the child owns the problem of not getting what she wants through a tantrum. Being ignored is the logical consequence for having a tantrum.

Find Out What Works Best for You

As you experiment with each of the skills you are learning, you will discover which ones work best with your children. For example, some children respond very well to reflective listening and I-messages, others don't. Consequences are effective with most children if applied correctly. Give each skill your full effort and try it often before deciding what works best for you.

Dealing with Typical Discipline Challenges

Misbehavior can be thought of as a game played according to rules designed by the child. In fact, the child is the only one who knows the rules. The rules involve the parent responding in an expected way, such as giving negative or undue attention, fighting or giving in, or getting his feelings hurt and retaliating. Responding in a way your child doesn't expect can stop the misbehavior game. Also, it is important to realize the child is discouraged. The child fails to recognize she can achieve belonging in useful ways and, therefore, she gains importance through misbehavior.

The following section discusses common behavior problems, some of the possible goals of the behavior, who owns the problem situation, and some alternatives for you to try that place responsibility for the behavior on your children. The goals given are only possibilities. Remember that you judge the goal based upon how you feel when the misbehavior happens and what the child does when you respond.

Morning Routine Problems

In many homes the morning routine of getting the children up, dressed, fed, and off to school is mayhem. There are many opportunities for attention getting and power plays in the morning routine. Dawdling, yelling, and fighting can start the day in an exciting way.

Many parents assume ownership of the children's problems in the morning routine. Why? Because they believe it is their responsibility to get the children off to school. The law does say that children of certain ages must be in school, but by assuming all of the responsibility for getting the children to school, the parents let themselves be trapped. The following two steps give responsibility to the children for their own morning routine problems.

- Get the children an alarm clock and show them how to set it. In a friendly way, tell them that they are old enough to get themselves up on time and off to school.
- Set a time for breakfast and tell family members that they have to be dressed and ready to leave the house before they can eat. If a child doesn't have time for breakfast, she'll have to skip it in order to be on time to school. Let the natural consequences of hunger do the teaching.

If a child misses her ride to school, she can walk if this is practical. If it is not practical to walk, she may have to stay home, if there is an adult home during the day. But tell your child that as far as you are concerned it is a school day, and you are going to assume she is in school. Pay no attention to her until the normal time she would be home from school. Do this in a matter-of-fact, not punitive, way. While the child may think staying home is fun at first, the enjoyment usually wears off when she receives no attention from you. If the school requires a written excuse note from you, simply write a note saying the child decided not to go to school that day and let the child deal with the consequences. If the problem persists, you may want to ask the attendance officer or principal to help you by coming to the house and taking the child to school.

If you drive the children to school and they aren't ready to go when you are, inform them in the evening that you will no longer be responsible for seeing they get ready on time. If they aren't dressed by a certain time, you'll assume they've decided to travel to school in an undressed state. You will put their clothes in a paper bag and they can dress in the car when you reach the school.

If you work outside the home and have a dawdler, you'll have to make some different arrangements. Depending on the age of the child, she can stay home alone or be driven to school, but for a while you may have to leave earlier than you usually do so you can get to work on time. While leaving early may be inconvenient, if you are patient the child will learn from such consequences as missing breakfast and having to dress in the car when she reaches school.

The important goal to keep in mind is to give the children responsibility for the morning routine with minimum involvement from you. Expect them to take responsibility for getting themselves up, dressed, to breakfast, and out the door. If they take their lunches, they can make them. They also can be responsible for collecting the things they need to take to school. Young school-aged children may need some help with dressing, lunches, and so on at first, but they, too, can learn to take responsibility.

It is important to inform the school if you expect problems with the children getting to school on time. Explain that you are trying to help the children learn to be responsible for their morning routine and ask for the school's help. Children who are late to school may have to make up the time, for example.

Conflicts over Children's Rooms
Children's rooms are often battle zones because the parents believe the room is part of the house or apartment and the children believe it's their own private residence. The attention getter will clean it when reminded, but the power seeker will stall forever.

If you are playing the messy room game, you have assumed responsibility for the child's problem—you are the one concerned about the condition of the room, not the child. Since children cherish their rooms, they believe they have a right to keep them the way they want them. You may not agree. Most children, however, will learn to put things away and clean up if the parent gets out of the room-tending business. The natural consequences of stepping on toys or losing things will do the teaching. Letting the natural consequences do the teaching requires stamina because it usually takes quite some time. Close the door if the room bothers you.

"But I just cleaned it!"

Young children can develop a sense of orderliness in their room if parents and children make playing "pick up" together an enjoyable way to spend time. But messiness has often been too well established for older children to learn from this approach.

Many families have at least one neat child and one sloppy child. Like other opposites in personality characteristics, these differences reveal the competition between siblings or stepsiblings. Getting after the sloppy child just reinforces the competition between the two.

If children share a room, let them work out how the room is to be kept. Often children with different standards will be in the same room. Stay out of the conflict. Some children have been known to draw lines down the middle of the room, each keeping her side the way she wants to keep it.

If dirt is being tracked into the rest of the house from a child's room, she will need to clean it up. Establish a time by when this will be done and expect it to be done.

Insults and Verbal Attacks

When a child attacks you verbally, the goal may be revenge. The child may say something similar to "I hate you!" "You don't love me!" "You made my father leave!" "You're not my real mother!" "You can't tell me what to do!"

The child owns this problem since he is the one who is upset. The attack may be a response to something the parent has done, and, of course, the parent owns the responsibility for her part in the conflict.

The first step in stopping the misbehavior is to examine your part in it. Have you provoked the attack? If so, apologize, use your reflective listening skills, and, if necessary, use I-messages and exploring alternatives to negotiate. If you feel the attack was unprovoked, you can choose to ignore the comments and with-draw from the scene. If necessary, discuss the problem at a later time when the child has calmed down. Or, if you can remain calm, use your communication skills to discuss the problem at the time it occurs.

Fights between Children

Many people believe arguing and fighting is a normal part of human nature, but actually it is learned and has a purpose. Children may learn arguing from observing parents and physical fighting from being spanked or observing siblings being spanked. Spanking teaches a physical solution to conflicts.

Arguing and fighting can serve the purpose of gaining attention from parents, overpowering parents ("You can't make us stop"), or getting even with parents, for example, by hitting the "favored" child. The most effective way for dealing with children's conflicts is to let both siblings and stepsiblings settle them on their own. Getting involved by playing judge, lecturing, or mediating reinforces children's goals of misbehavior.

It's not important who started the conflict; both children share responsibility for their involvement. Punishing the "guilty" party only reinforces the resentment and retaliation against you and the "innocent" child. Punishing both children leaves both ready to get even. Telling them fighting is wrong and that they should try to get along together falls on deaf ears. Trying to get

them to settle the conflict peacefully fails because of the angry feelings involved.

If children are not allowed to settle their own conflicts, how will they learn to get along with others? In a fight, for example, the natural consequence of being hit by a sibling can teach children not to hit the other children in the family. Many parents are reluctant to let their children fight physically for fear the children might hurt each other, but real harm does not usually occur in children's fights. However, if you think the children will harm each other, by all means separate them until they calm down. Do this in a firm, but not angry or accusing, way: "I'm afraid you guys may really hurt each other. Russ, you go in the living room and, Dennis, you go in the kitchen. When you have both calmed down and are willing to stop hitting, you can be together again if you want to be." If the fighting continues, increase the separation time with each occurrence. Evaluate carefully whether you need to intervene, because the fighting can be reinforced through your involvement.

If there is a large age difference between the fighting children and you feel the younger one will get hurt, resist the temptation to punish the older child. Simply remove the younger child and say something such as "It appears you are not ready to be with your sister today." Young children expect to be protected and gain power over the older children by getting the parents to punish the older ones. They do not expect to be removed from the situation. Even when age differences are small, younger children often manipulate parents into settling their conflicts with older children. Blaming and punishing the older child not only invites resentment and retaliation from the older one, it teaches the younger child to get others to take responsibility for his conflicts.

Some parents won't let girls and boys fight. They believe boys should not hit girls. Think of the power girls learn to use when parents protect them from their brothers. If a girl is going to involve herself in a physical fight, she too can learn from the consequences.

When parents first remove attention from children's conflicts, they often find the children trying to pull them back in. For example, a child may complain he's being picked on. When this happens, listen to the child's feelings and express confidence in his ability to handle the conflict. Say nothing to future complaints, or you will be involving yourself in the conflict. The frequency and intensity of your children's fights may increase as the children try to get your attention. But, as you remain firm in your resolve not to interfere and the children are convinced you are not going to get involved, the number of conflicts and their intensity usually lessens. Remove yourself physically from the noise—go to your bedroom or take a walk—anything to get your mind off their conflict. When this is impractical, offer your children the choice of stopping the fight or going elsewhere to do battle.

If a child really wants to talk about how she can get along with a sibling, offer to discuss the problem and explore alternatives. Children can also learn how to explore alternatives together as they participate in the family meetings.

Schoolwork Problems

School is a source of conflict in many homes, especially if education has a high value for parents. Not doing schoolwork or getting low grades is a perfect opportunity for children to gain attention, assert their power, or get even with parents and teachers.

Most parents want their children to do well in school. Many believe it's their responsibility to make sure the children study and learn. There are power conflicts over school issues in many homes, as parents find it's impossible to try to force an unmotivated child to learn. In fact, trying to force children to perform in school through reward or punishment usually increases the problem. Parents become discouraged as their youngsters don't perform to their expectations.

> Seventeen-year-old Laura is a capable student who doesn't perform to her potential. Her parents will not let her get a driver's learning permit until she makes the grades they expect she should have. Laura says she wants to drive, yet she doesn't get the required grades. Laura is unaware of being in a subtle power contest with her parents. Even though Laura wants to drive, she won't give her parents the satisfaction of meeting their demands.

If you have a reluctant student, it may be best for you to let the child experience the consequences the school provides for children who avoid doing schoolwork. You could discuss the problem with your child and explain that from now on school is his responsibility. Explain that you will provide assistance if the child really needs it, but that you realize you can't make him learn. Wish the child success and show interest when the child does his schoolwork, but stay out of the problem in other ways. The child is more likely to take responsibility for schoolwork if you don't reinforce his bids for attention, power, or revenge by becoming involved in school struggles. You must be firm in your decision to stay out of the problem as the child will not believe you and may try to pull you back in. Be sure you notify the school about your decision and your reasons for giving the child responsibility for his schooling. As you build your relationship with your child—concentrating on nonschool areas—chances are the child will feel better about himself and this increased self-esteem will carry over into the academic area.

Children who display inadequacy, on the other hand, need another approach. Focus on the child's strengths and find a good tutor who knows how to encourage children. Tutors can help with children who seek attention, power, or revenge if they are aware of the child's motivation and are good at working with such children.

It is always possible that your children could perform poorly because of an ineffective teacher. If you suspect this is the problem and meetings with the teacher are unsatisfactory, by all means discuss the issue with the principal. A change in teachers may be in order.

The most important thing to remember about discipline is that effective procedures are based on choice and mutual respect. Effective discipline helps the child learn to be self-disciplined and responsible as well as cooperative with others. The following chart summarizes for you the discipline problems discussed in this chapter and some possible solutions.

Encouragement is the most important ingredient in any discipline procedure. You may be rejecting the behavior, but you accept and care for the child. You have learned in this and previous chapters how to deal with almost any parent-child problem. In the next chapter, more personal and family challenges will be explored.

Activity Assignment

During the next week, use a logical consequence in a situation in which you believe it will be successful.

Chart 7. Common Discipline Problems and Possible Solutions

Problem	Possible Solution
Refusing to wear a coat	Let child experience natural consequence of being cold.
Refusing to eat what is served	Let child experience natural consequence of being hungry.
Not going to bed on time	Let child experience natural consequence of being tired.
Allowances	Give child enough to cover most expenses and let child experience logical consequence of having no money if child doesn't budget.
Chores	Distribute chores in family meeting and establish work-before-fun rule or logical consequences.
Homework and grades	Let child experience logical consequences given by school for not doing schoolwork. Help children who display inadequacy through tutors. Meet with teacher if you believe teaching is ineffective.
Morning routine problems	Give child responsibility of getting self off to school. If practical, child should walk when ride is missed. Do not write excuse note if child must stay home because of missed ride.
Conflicts over children's rooms	Give child responsibility for keeping room clean. Let natural consequences of stepping on things or losing things do the teaching.
Insults and verbal attacks	Apologize, use reflective listening, I-messages, and negotiation if you provoked attack. If attack was unprovoked, ignore, leave, and possibly discuss later.
Fights between children	Let children settle their own fights. Remove yourself physically or offer children choice of going elsewhere to fight or stopping.

Important Points to Remember in Chapter 7

1. Discipline is a learning experience designed to help children develop self-discipline. The discipline system in this book, called democratic discipline, is based on equality and mutual respect, choices within limits, and acceptance of responsibility for the consequences of one's choices.

2. Discipline involves both the prevention and correction of problems. Problems can be prevented by giving children control of their own lives in areas that they are ready to handle.

3. Natural and logical consequences replace reward and punishment as methods for correcting misbehavior. They permit children to choose their behavior within limits and be accountable for their choices.

4. A natural consequence involves the results of violating the law of nature. A logical consequence involves the results of violating the rules of cooperation.

5. Logical consequences have the following characteristics.

- They are designed to fit the needs of the situation.
- The parental action in the logical consequence fits the misbehavior.
- They deal with what will happen now and in the future as opposed to what happened in the past.
- They are often set up in advance in a firm, but friendly, way.
- They are based on mutual respect.
- They involve choices and accountability.

6. Do's and don'ts for using consequences include:

- Let children experience consequences.
- Replace talk with action.
- Phrase consequences respectfully.
- Put children all in the same boat.
- Remain friendly as well as firm.
- Be consistent.
- Don't yield to others' opinions.
- Don't dwell on the negative.

- Don't take on all problems at once.
- Don't create hidden intentions.

7. Spouses and ex-spouses often have different discipline styles. Conflicts over different styles can be dealt with constructively through the process of exploring alternatives. If agreement is not reached, agree to disagree.

8. Single parents need to handle discipline problems that occur between them and their children when they are with the children and not try to handle problems between the children and the other parent.

9. Stepfamily parents can handle discipline problems effectively when they follow these guidelines.

- The parents discuss what they expect from each other.
- The biological parent handles disciplinary problems except those that occur between the stepparent and the stepchildren.
- The stepparent makes every effort to establish a relationship with the children through spending time with them and being encouraging. The stepparent disciplines only when the children do something that interferes with the stepparent's rights.
- The biological parent gradually introduces the stepparent as a person who is equally responsible for discipline by telling the children the stepparent is in charge in the biological parent's absence.
- As the relationships in the family grow, parents share the responsibility for discipline and work at developing a consistent style.

10. If children complain that they can do something at their other parent's home that you don't allow, acknowledge that you are sure they enjoy the activity but state that you don't agree with it and change the subject.

11. Challenges in parenting are best met with some or all of the skills of reflective listening, I-messages, exploring alternatives, and consequences. You can decide what skills to use by:

- Considering the child's goal of misbehavior
- Deciding who owns the problem
- Finding out what works best for you

12. Some typical discipline problems that can be solved by placing more responsibility for their own behavior on children are:

- Morning routine problems
- Conflicts over children's rooms
- Insults and verbal attacks
- Fights between children
- Schoolwork problems

Chapter 8

Personal and Family Challenges

The preceding chapters have provided skills and concepts to help you meet the challenges of your new family structure. You are now ready to apply these ideas to special issues and challenges that may confront your family. This chapter will explore some of these special concerns.

Dealing with Criticism of Your Parenting Methods

Whenever you try new methods for dealing with family problems, you are bound to attract someone's attention. Usually the people who are most critical of the changes you make are least secure in their own parenting role. The person who criticizes may be a discouraged parent.

It is easy to overreact to criticism by assuming it is directed at your family structure. Each time you are tempted to doubt yourself and become overconcerned with criticism, take a moment to focus on the long-range goals you hope to accomplish through changing your parenting methods. Change takes time. Remember where you started and look at how far you have come. Encourage yourself by realizing that you are providing the building blocks that will eventually produce a mentally healthy, responsible adult.

Rosella's mother, Lucia, always spent several weeks a year with Rosella and her son, Tony. Since Rosella's husband had died, Lucia had constantly offered advice on how to discipline 9-year-old Tony. Rosella generally took her mother's advice because she

felt overwhelmed by the responsibility for disciplining that her husband had previously carried out. When Rosella decided to change her discipline style, Lucia became very critical. At dinner one evening, Tony threw a tantrum and Lucia got upset when Rosella ignored him. "Why don't you punish him?" she said. "You shouldn't let him act like that. Be a good mother now and straighten him out." Rosella ignored her mother's criticism and thought of her long-range goal of changing Tony's attention-seeking behavior. Although her mother thought her new ideas on discipline were foolish when Rosella explained them, Rosella kept using the new method and saw a gradual change in Tony's behavior.

If you consistently respond to criticism by focusing on your progress, you will experience an increase in self-confidence. You will also provide an encouraging model for the discouraged parent who offered the criticism. Through your example, people may find the courage to make necessary changes in their parenting methods. Use your reflective listening skills when someone criticizes you: "It seems you're disturbed about the way I'm handling this." Then state your own feelings in an I-message: "While my approach may not appeal to you, I believe that what I'm doing will help Richard develop a sense of responsibility."

Developing Your Sense of Humor

Learning to look at the humorous side of situations is basic to having satisfying relationships. Seeing the funny side of problems gives you more options for solving them and keeps small skirmishes from becoming full-fledged wars.

You may have to dig deep to find the humor in the stressful situations you face as a parent. It may be helpful to look at the problem as if you were a scriptwriter for a TV situation comedy. Take care, though, to use humor and not sarcasm. Children react to sarcasm as an insult and may intensify inappropriate behavior.

Parents who take the time to look for humor in their problems find a more relaxed home atmosphere and a reduction in disturbing incidents can be payoffs. The following example will give you an idea of how one parent used humor to solve a problem.

> Carol's new husband, Tom, is away during the week on business, leaving her in charge of the household and his 16-year-old son, Ben. In her eagerness to get Ben to like her, Carol has allowed him to take advantage of her. The way she deals with how he handles his paper route is one example of this.
>
> Her day begins with phone calls from Ben's irate customers. Ben has already left for school, so she feels she has to take care of the customers' problems. In an effort to be what she considers a "good mom," she delivers missed papers and takes messages, hoping Ben will do better tomorrow. Neither taking care of Ben's customers, nor nagging, coaxing, or lecturing has improved Ben's performance. She and Ben are in a power struggle and are angry much of the time.

Seething with anger one morning after receiving the usual quota of phone calls, Carol has a fantasy. She suddenly sees herself as a "supersecretary" who simultaneously handles irate customers, types, answers a dozen phones, and gets coffee for her boss. She fantasizes Ben as a lazy boss, who sleeps behind his desk while she manages the company. She decides to use this fantasy in a discussion with Ben and present her list of employee requirements at a time when she is no longer angry.

As Ben grumbles about his customers that evening, her moment arrives. Carol says, "Ben, I didn't realize I had applied for a secretarial job. If I'm going to accept the job, there are some things we need to negotiate. I have a list of employment issues we need to resolve. It includes salary, working conditions, grievance procedures, job description, insurance, expense money, workman's compensation, withholding taxes, social security, sick leave, and paid vacation. Also, I'll need a desk and chair, some notepads and pencils, and a push-button phone with a recorder and two lines. Shall we start with the equipment or the employee benefits?"

After they have had a good laugh, Carol states what she really plans to do to get out of the power struggle: "Ben, I'm confident you can handle your customers. So starting tomorrow I'll tell any customer who calls to call back after 5:00 when you will be home."

In the foregoing example, Carol has demonstrated two important concepts. The first is that most situations have a comical side. Waiting to discuss a problem until after your anger subsides is the second.[1] When she didn't do what Ben expected (nag and fight), Carol changed the mood of their discussions and ended the stalemate.

Improving Communication between Ex-spouses

"If natural parents can be civil to each other or, better yet, friendly and comfortable, the children have much less need to choose sides. When ex-spouses are friendly, the children do not experience the trauma of going back and forth between two armed camps."[2] The preceding statement describes two of the most important reasons for improving communication with your ex-spouse: eliminating the possibility of children choosing sides and reducing the frictions that occur when children are members in two households.

It is very difficult to have friendly communications with anyone when you are involved in a conflict. It's even more difficult to communicate effectively with an ex-spouse because of the feelings of betrayal that often surround the end of an intimate relationship. Extended family members who take sides can add to the unpleasantness. *The Parents Without Partners Sourcebook* suggests this problem is best handled by agreeing to communicate only as parents (not as spouses), keeping the best interests of the children as your goal in any exchange.[3]

Resolving Conflicts in Private
After their parents divorce, most children side with one parent and blame the other for the divorce but continue to worry

about the response of the parent they blame. In the interests of self-preservation, children usually side with the parent with the power, the custodial parent.

Children view themselves as the center of the universe, which for them is defined as the family. Since many children believe their behavior was the basis for the conflicts leading to the divorce, it is essential they do not continue to see themselves as the source of conflict between their parents. The mistaken guilt they feel about their part in the marital breakup is increased by parental fights.

Most children recognize that the divorce has placed them in a very powerful position. They are the primary reason for any continued involvement between the parents. Some children mistakenly use this power to manipulate parents to create conflicts in both households. You may recognize this divide-and-conquer technique in the following example.

One of the major issues leading to Franklin and Letitia's divorce was continued disagreement over how to discipline the children. Franklin felt Letitia was too strict, and she felt he was too lenient. They constantly undermined each other's discipline methods in front of the children. The children often used these disagreements to effectively manipulate both parents.

In the best interests of the children, the divorce decree stipulated joint physical and legal custody with coparenting responsibilities. Unfortunately, at the time of the divorce, both Franklin and Letitia were so angry they failed to spell out the details of how this was to be implemented. The following months brought many confrontations based on their old disagreements about discipline.

Eight-year-old Ladonna and 6-year-old Tiffany were experts at playing divide and conquer. They quickly recognized their power to keep the fight going and to be in control. The first things Franklin heard when he picked them up at Letitia's apartment were complaints about her strictness. Each time the girls returned to Letitia's place, they greeted her discipline attempts with the refrain "Dad doesn't make us do that. His house is neat. We can do anything we want." Each time Ladonna and Tiffany moved, the parents would have a confrontation about what the girls had said regarding discipline or the lack of it. The parents experienced tension and dread each time the girls were to switch homes.

Franklin and Letitia need to resolve their discipline conflicts in private and present a united front to the girls. If they don't they will be teaching Ladonna and Tiffany a negative skill—how to manipulate people to create conflict and friction. When they agree to resolve their differences privately, the children will realize that their manipulation does not work anymore and will find more constructive ways to cooperate.

Ex-spouses do not have to agree on everything. If they did agree, they probably wouldn't have sought a divorce. They can learn to agree as parents on the important long-range goals they wish to achieve regarding the children. These goals can be negotiated through the steps for exploring alternatives found in Chapter 6. Once these goals are established, parents can work cooperatively. This cooperative arrangement will work best when conflicts are resolved in private, and you avoid listening to tattling about your ex-spouse.

Communicating Instead of Judging

It may be difficult for you not to criticize your ex-spouse if you feel hurt and betrayed. Often there is also an element of fear in criticism of an ex-spouse, fear of losing the children's love to the ex-spouse. When people feel vulnerable, they tend to judge rather than communicate, misinterpret others' intentions, and blow problems out of proportion. Criticizing your ex-spouse with your children can have negative consequences for your relationship with them.

> Brenda's ex-spouse, Mark, brings the children home late one Sunday. She knows they have been to the zoo, a ball game, a circus, and to visit her ex-sister-in-law, who can't stand her. The explanation Mark offers about freeway traffic and dinner being late at his sister's house sounds like an excuse to Brenda. Her first thought is "He's just as thoughtless as he always was." She tells Mark this and he responds angrily, "You never want the kids to enjoy being with me." The children chime in, criticizing Brenda and protecting Mark. The next weekend that Mark has custody of the children, he brings them home late on purpose.

What might have happened if Brenda had withheld judgment and tried a different approach? In the next example, Brenda uses some communication techniques discussed earlier.

When Mark explained that he was late because of traffic and his sister's dinner, Brenda listened for his feelings. Instead of being angry and attacking—which is what he expected—she said, "Sounds like you were really worried about being late." Her remark opened the door for further discussion, which ended with an agreement by Mark to call when he would be late bringing the children home so Brenda would not worry. The children, therefore, did not feel the need to choose sides, and it was likely Mark would not be late again.

No one goes through life without making mistakes. Today's judge may be tomorrow's defendant. The person who communicates rather than judges usually finds the "golden rule" works in everyone's favor.

Living Your Life Apart from Being a Parent

Being a parent is only one of the many roles that you play. When you invest all of your energy in this role, equating your self-worth with the success or failure of your children and ignoring the other roles you can play, you limit your options. It is wise to spend time on personal growth by developing other aspects of your life. To do this, you will need to re-evaluate your view of the proper use of time.

Most people see time as an enemy. They complain about their lack of time and often feel overwhelmed by the number of tasks to be completed on a given day. Usually people fail to see that they have the power to control the way they manage time.

In order to meet the challenges of the new family structure, it is essential that you make time for yourself. This is not a selfish desire, but a basic physical and psychological necessity. Your mind and body need time to replenish the energy needed to meet daily challenges. Noncustodial parents, too, who may feel they have too much time, must plan for personal growth in roles other than the parental role.

Managing time creatively requires you to look at goals and priorities rather than just tasks and time. For the moment, put aside your usual daily "to do" list and think about the goals you want to accomplish this year. As you make your list, be sure to include personal goals, such as learn to ski, make two new friends, invite people for dinner, or spend a weekend each month with my spouse. Next, prioritize your goals; decide what is your most important goal, your second most important goal, and so on. Be sure to give personal goals equal weight with other important goals. Now break each goal up into manageable blocks of time—such as daily, weekly, monthly—required for its completion. For example, if your goal is to run in a 5-mile race in 6 months, you may set a daily goal of running for ½ hour a day, a weekly goal of increasing your total distance each week by a mile, and a 3-month goal of running in a 2-mile race. Finally, meet with other family members to get their input and cooperatively make up a new "to do" list for accomplishing daily chores needed to keep the family functioning. By involving the family in daily chores, you will have some free time for personal goals.

At first you may find it is difficult to give personal goals the same priority as other commitments. You may even feel guilty. If you do feel guilty, remind yourself, "I'll be a better parent if I take time for myself. I'll have more energy and tolerance." Making a commitment to take time for yourself—whether it involves dinner with friends or simply sitting and doing nothing—is a necessity not a luxury!

Sexuality

Loss of sexual confidence is a normal occurrence following divorce. While newly divorced parents may feel they need to prove themselves sexually attractive, playing musical bed partners can cause children to worry about being replaced. It is wise to shield children from casual affairs to reduce the possibility of their becoming insecure and jealous. Many children are confused if you invite casual partners to stay overnight. In their experience, parents are people who sleep together.

When it is apparent the relationship is one of commitment, the children need to be informed. It is important that they have time to adjust to the proposed change in the family structure and understand that your new spouse will share your bed. Now is the time to be frank about the relationship you will share as a couple. While this may seem obvious to you, remember that the children still have fantasies about your ex-spouse returning. Many a parent has been dismayed to return from the honeymoon and find the children incensed at the idea of the new stepparent sharing a bed with their parent.[4]

Keeping Your Children Safe when They Are Home Alone

The safety and psychological well-being of children who spend part of each day at home unsupervised have become major worries for parents and the community. When your working schedule necessitates that the children come home to an empty house, your primary concern is usually for their safety. "How can they be protected if I'm not there?" is a question that is always on your mind. The second question often is, "How do I convince them to keep the door locked without scaring them to death?" Both of these questions are related to what you do about the house key. Chapter 6 gave an example about how to handle this.

Many children at home alone or with siblings are afraid but are reluctant to tell their parents. They also are concerned about how to handle emergencies, are usually lonely, and may feel isolated from their friends because they can't leave the house.[5] In *The Parents Without Partners Sourcebook,* Dr. Thomas J. Long addresses these concerns with the following suggestions.[6]

- If possible, don't leave children under age 10 home alone and don't leave those over age 10 alone for more than 2½ hours.
- Instead of putting your oldest child in charge of the other children, assign tasks directly to each child and have each child report to you.
- Call your children periodically or have them call you when they are home. This shows that you're thinking of them. There may be a telephone service in your area of the country that children can call when they are home alone and feel lonely.
- Instruct your children in what to say when they answer the telephone. You may want them to say something such as "Mom is in the shower" or "Dad has company right now. Can he call you back?" You could also use a special code (for example, two rings, hang up, and call again) so that your child will know it's you calling. Codes can also prevent your child from going with anyone who does not use the code. (For example, an authorized person might say, "I'm from Bluebird.")
- Help your children build a stable routine. Regular responsibilities, a set time to watch television, and an occasional visit to a friend help to do this. Pets, especially dogs, can provide both safety and companionship.

- Try to get home at the same time each day. If you are late, your children may feel abandoned. Leave work on time and don't stop for errands. Pick up your children and take them with you if you need to run errands. If you know you'll be late, call and reassure your children and give an alternate time when you'll be home.
- Ask neighbors if your children can contact them in an emergency. The Parent Watch Program, sponsored by many PTAs, provides stickers for parents who are home after school to place in a window. Children can go to one of these homes for help. Don't be embarrassed to ask your neighbor for help. Perhaps you can do something in exchange for your neighbor's looking out for your child after school. You might want to pay an adult to be available. Assure your child that this is one adult it is OK to approach.

Jeff's parents get home from work 3 hours after he is home from school. Ten-year-old Jeff knew that he could always visit the next-door neighbor, Sandy, if something was wrong or he was lonesome. He often went to her house in the afternoon and sometimes ate dinner with Sandy and her 2-year-old. Jeff's parents were able to help Sandy by giving her rides to the grocery store and laundromat.

The school is a community institition and, as such, has an investment in your child's welfare. Depending on how your community views the use of school facilities, you may want to request the use of a classroom when school is not in session. With the principal's assistance, you can contact interested parents and develop a program to fit the needs of working parents. Parents who have implemented this kind of program often find that retired people, nonworking parents, teachers with similar child-care problems, teachers in training, and older teens are willing volunteers.

Resolving Custody Issues

Custody of your children probably is the most important and difficult divorce issue you will have to resolve. The custody provisions of the divorce decree will affect every area of your life—time, finances, housing, recreation, family relationships, and so on. Therefore, it is prudent to take time to iron out differences, spell out specifics, and let tempers cool before asking the court to make it legal.

Laws protect children against abuse, kidnapping, disease, neglect, and ignorance. However, there are no laws to protect against the abuses that happen to them in court custody battles. Children often receive the same treatment as houses, cars, and furniture; they are viewed as property to be divided between the parents. The psychological problems they incur are not recognized because most lawyers and judges have no training in human relations or child development. Therefore, it is up to the divorcing parents to ensure that the proposed custody arrangements are both workable and in the best interests of the children.

There are advantages and disadvantages to every form of custody arrangement. Sole custody (usually granted to the mother) has been the traditional form awarded by the court. However, the coparenting method—which seems to have the greatest benefits for children when both parents are able to set differences aside and work cooperatively—increasingly is being recognized as a viable option. Even though family law statutes vary from state to state, common sense does not. Therefore, it is important to take time to consider which form of custody is best for your children.

Most problems with custody occur because the participants are living in an unnatural situation devised by the court to mandate a solution to a family problem. This mandate is called a divorce decree and, like a contract, can only be renegotiated not appealed.

Experts in the fields of law, family counseling, divorce mediation, and social services believe many of the custody problems that are serious enough to come to their attention could have been avoided. The reason for most of these problems lies in the nonspecific nature of divorce decrees; they do not spell out specific details of who is responsible for what and how the children's time is to be shared.

If you are experiencing problems with the custody provisions of your divorce, renegotiate these issues with your ex-spouse. This involves a discussion of the current custody provisions in which each of you spells out those things that are working and those things that are not. Everything to be discussed should be well thought out and listed in writing so you will not be tempted to deviate and rehash old disagreements. Choose a time for discussion when both of you are calm and agree that all decisions should be made in light of "what is in the best interests of the children." If you find it impossible to renegotiate custody issues with your ex-spouse, secure the help of a divorce mediator. When agreement has been reached, you can both request the modifications be legalized.

Sole Custody

This form of custody gives all the rights, duties, and obligations regarding all aspects of the children's lives—social, emotional, physical, and psychological—to one parent. The other parent may be granted visitation rights, but all legal rights belong to the custodial parent. In effect, this means the noncustodial parent has no more rights than a family friend. The noncustodial parent cannot sign a report card or obtain medical treatment for the child without the custodial parent's permission.

Prior to the twentieth century, custody was traditionally granted to the father. However, the majority of custody awards (85 percent) since the early 1900s have been made to women. This shift from father to mother as custodial parent occurred because of formulation of the "Tender Years Doctrine." The doctrine was based on psychological literature that held mothers to be better suited than fathers to be guardians of young children. Acceptance of this doctrine by the courts largely excluded fathers from obtaining custody.[7]

In recent years, increasing numbers of fathers have asserted their rights and fought for custody of their children. As noncustodial parents they had virtually no rights and a large measure of financial responsibility. They felt deprived of the enjoyment of being with their children on a daily basis and desired to be nurturers—not just money machines.

Joint Custody/Coparenting

Until recently, one parent often had physical custody and the other had legal custody of the children. Neither had both. A form of joint custody, coparenting, refers to an arrangement in which the court awards the legal and physical custody of the children equally to both parents.

To make coparenting work, the parents have to agree to put aside their hostility and place the child's interests first, cooperate on division of time and responsibilities, and share equally in the legal responsibility. In this arrangement nobody wins and nobody loses. The continuity of the child's life is maintained at a difficult time. And, the child does not have to fear abandonment by one of the parents.

The major disadvantage of coparenting is that its implementation relies on the good will of two people who disagreed enough to get divorced. For this reason, many family courts are skeptical of parents who choose this option. Therefore, people who decide to opt for the coparenting form of joint custody are wise to involve a mediator. A skilled mediator who is not emotionally involved is able to look at the situation objectively and help the parents develop a detailed plan for realistic implementation of the court decree. The mediator is able to reduce confrontation between parents at a vulnerable time and convince the court that what the parents have decided is a carefully thought out plan in the best interest of the child.

Noncustodial Parents

Being a noncustodial parent can be upsetting and often leads to depression. While the custodial parent and the children often remain in the family home, the noncustodial parent not only loses a home but also becomes a visitor with few legal rights. Losing legal rights to the children does not include loss of the obligation to pay for their support. Most noncustodial parents find that the same court that harasses them for nonpayment of support will not enforce their visitation rights.

Many noncustodial parents cannot bear the pain of their status and simply disappear from their children's lives. Others attempt to bargain with the custodial parent by using child support as a weapon. Most noncustodial parents fear the loss of their children's love and attempt to buy the love with gifts, weekend trips, and permissiveness. These attempts usually meet with failure and increased hostility from the custodial parent.

Some noncustodial parents find they have a better relationship with their children than they did before the divorce. When they are free of the stresses of an unsatisfactory marriage, these parents find they are able to devote more time to developing a closer parent-child relationship.

> Throughout their marriage, Alice had expected Nick to deal with major discipline issues. It was not unusual for Nick to return from a business trip and be greeted at the door with: "You have to talk to Yvonne. I can't handle her anymore." As a single parent, Nick chose to no longer play the role of disciplinarian. Yvonne was used to relating to Nick as a critical absentee parent. However, after some initial suspicion, Yvonne opened up, and they developed a closer relationship.

A noncustodial parent who is not accustomed to spending a lot of time with the child may find it helpful initially to plan activities that do not involve a lot of talking. The parent may even want to include one of the child's friends on the first few outings. When the noncustodial parent and child are more comfortable in their new roles, they will find that communication between them is easier.[8]

The extended family of noncustodial parents is often overlooked in custody agreements. Grandparents' visitation rights are becoming a legislative issue in many states. Grandparents, aunts, uncles, and cousins retain the same relationship to your children even though your spouse may be "ex" to you. The extended family can provide continuity and be a source of support and love for you and the children as you build a new family structure. Even if you have serious disagreements with your ex-spouse's family, it is a mistake to assume these disagreements extend to the children. Cutting the children off from loving family members only adds to their feelings of loss.

Dealing with the School

Schools do make a conscious effort to meet the needs of children and families. However, like the rest of the community, they are often confused about who is considered to be a parent in the new family structure. It is up to the custodial parent to let the school know whether they should send notices to, or be in contact with, the ex-spouse and in the case of remarriage, the stepparent.

> Liling is graduating from high school and what should be a happy time has become a hassle. Her school has a policy that each student may have only two guests present at graduation and has sent the invitation to her mother as the parent of record. Liling has developed a good relationship with her stepfather, who assumes he is included in the invitation. Liling also has a close relationship with her father and stepmother and does not want to hurt them. How does she decide who should get the tickets for her graduation?

Both children and the parent or stepparent are often unhappy when a parent is left out of school activities through oversight. The child may feel the parent doesn't care, and the parent may feel excluded. Many schools unwittingly leave out a parent or stepparent and are happy to cooperate when informed. You can keep this from happening and use the opportunity to educate the school about the realities facing today's families. Make sure biological parents and stepparents are included in the school's records as parents of record. In this way, everyone's needs will be met.

Parents have an excellent opportunity to educate teachers and school personnel and create new expectations. For example, in response to a negative school conference, parents can point out that research shows family structure is not a predictor of school performance.[9]

Most parents experience times when it is impossible to attend a school function. Developing a network of friends who will serve as stand-ins is one approach for handling extracurricular activities requiring parental attendance. You will have many opportunities to pay back those who helped you out.

Preventing Kidnapping

Many missing children are believed to have been taken by their noncustodial parent. This is a revealing commentary on the problems inherent in many custody situations. Parents who kidnap their own children usually only do so as a last resort. Divorced parents who cooperate in coparenting do not experience this kind of problem.

Some children are also kidnapped because of the lack of adoptable children or for other reasons. Law enforcement agencies recommend all parents keep up-to-date photographs, videotapes, and fingerprints of their children. This is particularly important for noncustodial parents of young children who live a distance from the custodial parent. When a small child disappears far from home, crucial time may be lost if the noncustodial parent does not have a current picture.

Parents can also help their children be aware of the dangers of accepting rides or gifts from strangers. Criminals look for a child who is alone, trusting, compliant, and respects adults. The Adam Walsh Child Resource Center recommends you help your child become "street smart" by doing the following things:[10]

1. Teach them what a stranger is. You can do this by teaching them who is safe—a policeman, neighbor, teacher, store clerk, etc.

2. Don't dress them differently from their peers. Criminals look for children who wear expensive clothing.

3. Teach them to travel in a group. There is safety in numbers.

4. Teach them about safe places along their route where they can go for assistance.

5. Teach them not to take shortcuts and to stick to a regular route.

6. Tell them to trust their instincts. If a situation does not feel right they should leave immediately.

7. Tell them they should run away fast to a crowded place if they feel threatened.

8. Most important, teach them it's okay to say no. Polite children who respect adults need to be told they have your permission and support to say no to adults when they feel something is wrong.

As discussed earlier, code words can be used to identify appropriate persons, and the help of a neighborhood watch program can be enlisted. A code word is not to be shared with anyone. If you feel the code word is no longer secret, change it.

Teach your children to never open the door to anyone unless that person knows the code word. Whenever possible, call the children and inform them if you have asked someone to come to the house while you aren't home. Under no circumstances are they to open the door to a stranger or let that person know you aren't home. Provide the children with a script, such as "Dad can't come to the door right now, but you can leave a note on

"Thank for calling, Mom, but you're supposed to answer
'Captain Kirk' when I say 'Mr. Spock'!"

the porch." Many parents instruct their children to call them or a neighbor if the children feel uncomfortable or the stranger is persistent.

Rehearse with your child how to handle situations involving strangers. You can do this by inventing some situations and asking your child to tell you how she would handle it. Be sure to allow sufficient time to explore all the possibilities and feel sure that both you and the child understand what she is going to do. Not knowing what to do terrifies children. Knowledge gives them confidence and promotes safety.

Preventing Dissolution of the Stepfamily

Some stepfamilies do not deal with problems until they become crises. Sometimes a crisis forces decisions and change resulting in a stronger family bond. However, unwillingness to resolve a crisis may result in divorce.

Regardless of whether you function well in crisis or not, waiting for a crisis to occur before settling family differences may be compared to neglecting to have the car serviced until the transmission falls out. The effects of stress and the possibility of deteriorating relationships are increased and you may not be able to repair the relationships.

The impact of another divorce and the loss that entails can be catastrophic for children. They may lose not only the stepfamily but the stepfamily's extended family as well.

The key to saving a stepfamily involves a resolution of the immediate crisis and a definite plan for how to handle future conflicts. Three techniques for crisis proofing the family are: use the family meeting as a tool to encourage discussion of issues and concerns; deal with conflicts before they reach the crisis point (seeking professional help when necessary); and listen to each other's feelings.

Dealing with Substance Abuse

Substance abuse affects may families today, including some single-parent families and stepfamilies. If your ex-spouse is a substance abuser, you face a unique challenge. You are not the person to confront your ex-spouse. Substance abusers will use anything to avoid the truth; your ex-spouse will use the disagreements that led you to seek divorce as part of the denial that surrounds the problem. To break through this denial, you need a competent intervention specialist. This person is knowledgeable about the substance, knows how to get the abuser to seek treatment for addiction, knows the games and denial your ex-spouse will attempt to use, and is an impartial party. The intervention specialist will tell you how to proceed in terms of the abuser, yourself, and the children. Help in resolving this problem is usually only a phone call away.

Call upon an intervention specialist to help your current spouse also or any other member of the family who may be a substance abuser. Substance abuse affects every member of the abuser's family. Therefore, it is important to seek professional help to enable the whole family, not only the abuser, to get well.

This chapter has introduced you to a number of personal and family challenges and some possible solutions. These are summarized for you in the following chart.

Throughout this book, you have encountered a number of new ideas and skills regarding how to become a more effective parent and how to develop your interests and self-esteem outside of parenting, too. As you look back over the past few weeks, you can be encouraged by what you have learned and by the progress you've made. However, you may find that not all of your parenting challenges turn out the way you would like. You may at times forget to be encouraging or forget to use other new parenting skills. Like any newly acquired skill or idea, effective parenting techniques require study and practice in order to work for you. Practice the skills you have learned and review the concepts in the chapters.

And remember to have the courage to be imperfect; mistakes are part of learning and living. The support of an understanding friend or family member can help you as you learn and grow. If you are in a parenting group, you may find it helpful to develop a

Chart 8. Personal and Family Challenges and Possible Solutions

Challenge	Possible Solution
Dealing with criticism of your parenting method	Don't overreact. Focus on your progress. Use your reflective listening skills.
Developing your sense of humor	Look at situations as though you were a scriptwriter for a TV situation comedy. Use humor, not sarcasm.
Improving communication with your ex-spouse	Resolve conflicts in private. Communicate instead of judging.
Living your life apart from being a parent	Make time for yourself. Give personal goals the same priority as other commitments. Shield children from casual sexual affairs.
Keeping your children safe when they are home alone	Give children guidelines for handling house key, activities, and answering the phone. Arrange supervised before-and-after-school activities.
Resolving custody issues	Negotiate custody issues with your ex-spouse and, if necessary, a mediator.
Dealing with the school	Make sure biological parents and stepparents are included in school's records as parents of record.
Preventing kidnapping	Cooperate in coparenting with ex-spouse. Use a code word. Teach children to practice safety when they are out alone and how to answer the door when you aren't home.
Preventing dissolution of the stepfamily	Don't wait until a crisis to settle family differences.
Dealing with substance abuse	Get help for the substance abuser and the rest of the family.

relationship with another group member or plan for occasional group reunion meetings to check on each other's progress and provide encouragement. Whatever your situation, remember that you are not alone: other *New Beginnings* families like yours are experiencing the challenges and joys of working toward more effective parent-child relationships.

Activity Assignment

During the next week, think of one thing you have learned from this book and how you will continue to use it.

Important Points to Remember in Chapter 8

1. When you try new parenting methods you are bound to be criticized. Remember that:

- The person criticizing may be a discouraged parent.
- Your focus is on long-range goals you hope to accomplish.
- You have come a long way from where you started.

2. The ability to see the humorous side of a negative situation provides you with more options for solving problems.

3. Two of the most important reasons for improving communication with your ex-spouse are: eliminating the possibility of children choosing sides, and reducing the friction when children are members in two households.

4. Resolve your conflicts with your ex-spouse in private so the children will not have the power to manipulate you and your ex-spouse.

5. The person who communicates rather than judges usually finds the "golden rule" works in everyone's favor.

6. Spend time on personal growth. You won't always be a full-time parent.

7. Shield children from your casual sexual affairs and prepare them for your sexual relationship with your new spouse.

8. Keep children safe when they are home alone by:

- Giving them guidelines for handling the house key, activities, and answering the phone and door
- Arranging supervised before- and after-school activities

9. There is no ideal custody arrangement. Sole custody gives all rights, duties, and obligations regarding the children to one parent and leaves the other parent with no rights. Coparenting relies on the good will of the parents to work together for the best interests of the children. Select the custody arrangement that works best for everyone involved.

10. Some noncustodial parents become upset and depressed about their status. Others find that they have a better relationship with their children than they did before the divorce.

11. Single parents and stepfamily parents need to educate school personnel about the realities facing today's families.

12. Many missing children have been kidnapped by their noncustodial parent. The key to reducing this problem is cooperative coparenting. Teaching children how to deal with strangers also can help prevent kidnapping.

13. Dissolution of the stepfamily can be prevented by resolving problems before they reach the crisis point.

14. Substance abuse affects every member of the abuser's family. Professional help can enable the entire family to recover.

Notes

Notes for Chapter 1

1. Karen Diegmuller, "Divorce Exacts Its Price from Parent and Child Alike," *Insight* 2, no. 41 (1986): 14-17.
2. *Viewer's Guide for NBC White Paper: Divorce is Changing America* (June 3, 1986). (Available from CIStems, Inc., P. 0. Box 786, Madison Square Station, New York, NY 10159).
3. Emily B. Visher and John S. Visher, *Stepfamilies: A Guide to Working with Stepparents and Stepchildren* (New York: Brunner/Mazel, 1979).
4. *Viewer's Guide*, 1986.
5. Diegmuller, 1986.
6. Robert Brassington, "The Changing Family Constellation in Single Parent Families," *Individual Psychology* 38, no. 4 (December 1982): 369-379.
7. Visher & Visher, 1979.
8. Ibid.
9. Ibid.

Notes for Chapter 2

1. Don Dinkmeyer, *The Basics of Self-Acceptance* (Coral Springs, FL: CMTI Press, 1977).
2. Don Dinkmeyer and Lewis Losoncy, *The Encouragement Book* (Englewood Cliffs, NJ: Prentice-Hall, 1980).
3. Rudolf Dreikurs, *Social Equality: The Challenge of Today* (Chicago: Henry Regnery, 1971).
4. Alfred Adler, *Individual Psychology* (Patterson, NJ: Littlefield, Adams, 1959).

Notes for Chapter 3

1. Robert Brassington, "The Changing Family Constellation in Single Parent Families," *Individual Psychology* 38, no. 4 (December 1982): 369-379.

2. Elizabeth Einstein, *The Stepfamily: Living, Loving, and Learning* (New York: Macmillan, 1982).

3. Paul Druckman cited in Erna Paris, *Stepfamilies: Making Them Work* (New York: Avon, 1984).

4. Don Dinkmeyer and Jon Carlson, *Training in Marriage Enrichment* (Circle Pines, MN: American Guidance Service, 1984).

5. Rudolf Dreikurs and Vicki Soltz, *Children: The Challenge* (New York: Hawthorn, 1964).

6. Don Dinkmeyer and Gary D. McKay, *Systematic Training for Effective Parenting: The Parent's Handbook* (Circle Pines, MN: American Guidance Service, 1982, rev. ed.).

Notes for Chapter 4

1. Nira Kefir and Raymond Corsini, "Dispositional Sets: A Contribution to Typology," *Journal of Individual Psychology* (November 30, 1974): 163-178.

2. Alfred Adler, *Individual Psychology* (Patterson, NJ: Littlefield, Adams, 1959).

3. Albert Ellis and Robert A. Harper, *A New Guide to Rational Living* (Englewood Cliffs, NJ: Prentice-Hall, 1975).

4. Rudolf Dreikurs and Vicki Soltz, *Children: The Challenge* (New York: Hawthorn, 1964).

5. Edith A. Dewey, *Basic Applications of Adlerian Psychology* (Coral Springs, FL: CMTI Press, 1978).

6. Elizabeth Kübler-Ross, *On Death and Dying* (New York: Macmillan, 1969).

7. Ellis & Harper, 1975.

8. Herbert Benson, *Beyond the Relaxation Response* (New York: New York Times Book, 1984).

9. Edward A. Charlesworth and Ronald G. Nathan, *Stress Management: A Comprehensive Guide to Wellness* (New York: Ballantine, 1984).

Notes for Chapter 5

1. Thomas Gordon, *Parent Effectiveness Training* (New York: Peter H. Wyden, 1970).

2. Ibid.

3. Ibid.

Notes for Chapter 6

1. Rudolf Dreikurs and Loren Grey, *A Parent's Guide to Child Discipline* (New York: Hawthorn, 1970).

Notes for Chapter 7

1. *Webster's New World Dictionary* (New York: Simon & Schuster, 1984): 401.
2. Don Dinkmeyer and Gary D. McKay, *Systematic Training for Effective Parenting of Teens: The Parent's Guide* (Circle Pines, MN: American Guidance Service, 1983): 5.
3. Rudolf Dreikurs and Vicki Soltz, *Children: The Challenge* (New York: Hawthorn, 1964).
4. Don Dinkmeyer, Gary D. McKay, Don Dinkmeyer, Jr., James S. Dinkmeyer, and Joyce L. McKay, *The Next STEP: Effective Parenting Through Problem Solving* (Circle Pines, MN: American Guidance Service, 1987).
5. Dreikurs & Soltz, 1964.
6. Emily B. Visher and John S. Visher, *Stepfamilies: A Guide to Working with Stepparents and Stepchildren* (New York: Brunner/Mazel, 1979).
7. Linda Albert, *Coping with Kids* (New York: E. P. Dutton, 1982).
8. Ibid.

Notes for Chapter 8

1. Peter G. Jolin, *How to Succeed as a Stepparent* (New York: New American Library, 1983).
2. Emily B. Visher and John S. Visher, *Stepfamilies: A Guide to Working with Stepparents and Stepchildren* (New York: Brunner/Mazel, 1979): 168.
3. Stephen L. Atlas, *The Parents Without Partners Sourcebook* (Philadelphia: Running Press, 1984).
4. Elizabeth Einstein, *The Stepfamily: Living, Loving, and Learning* (New York: Macmillan, 1982).
5. Atlas, 1984.
6. Thomas J. Long cited in Atlas, 1984.
7. Erna Paris, *Stepfamilies: Making Them Work* (New York: Avon, 1984).
8. Fitzhugh Dodson and Ann Alexander, *Your Child: Birth to Age Six* (New York: Fireside, 1986).

9. Visher & Visher, 1979.

10. HBO Documentary, *How to Raise a Street-Smart Child* (1987) based on book of the same title by Grace Hechinger.

Index

About the Authors

Don Dinkmeyer

Dr. Don Dinkmeyer is President of Communication and Motivation Training Institute in Coral Springs, Florida. He received his Ph.D. in Counseling Psychology from Michigan State University in 1958. He holds a Diplomate in Counseling Psychology and a Diplomate in Marriage and Family Therapy. Dr. Dinkmeyer is a certified psychologist and a Fellow of the American Psychological Association. He maintains a private practice in marriage and family therapy.

Dr. Dinkmeyer has written over 125 professional articles and is the coauthor of many books including: *Systematic Training for Effective Parenting* (STEP), *Systematic Training for Effective Parenting of Teens* (STEP/Teen), *Systematic Training for Effective Teaching* (STET), *PREP for Effective Family Living*, *The Next STEP: Effective Parenting through Problem Solving*, *Raising a Responsible Child*, *The Encouragement Book*, and *Systems of Family Therapy*.

Dr. Dinkmeyer is a former teacher and counselor and an international educational and psychological consultant. He has conducted workshops on human relations and group leadership training in 46 states in the United States and in Canada, Mexico, South America, Europe, Great Britain, and Japan.

Gary D. McKay

Dr. Gary D. McKay is President of Communication and Motivation Training Institute-West in Tucson, Arizona. He received his Ph.D. in Counseling and Guidance from the University of Arizona in 1976. Dr. McKay is a certified psychologist, clinical member of the American Association for Marriage and Family Therapy, and a marriage and family therapist in private practice.

He is the coauthor with Don Dinkmeyer and others of *Systematic Training for Effective Parenting* (STEP), *Systematic Training for Effective Parenting of Teens* (STEP/Teen), *Systematic Training for Effective Teaching* (STET), *PREP for Effective Family Living*, *The Next STEP: Effective Parenting through Problem Solving*, and *Raising a Responsible Child*.

Dr. McKay is a former teacher and counselor and an international educational and psychological consultant. He has conducted workshops on human relations and group leadership training in the United States, Canada, Mexico, Europe, and Great Britain.

Joyce L. McKay

Dr. Joyce L. McKay is Vice-president of Communication and Motivation Training Institute-West in Tucson, Arizona. She received her Ph.D. in Counseling and Guidance from the University of Arizona in 1986. Dr. McKay is a marriage and family and career counselor in private practice. She is the coauthor with Don Dinkmeyer, Gary D. McKay, and others of *The Next STEP: Effective Parenting through Problem Solving*.

Dr. McKay is the former Director of the Pima County Developmental Career Guidance Project and Chairperson of the Governor's Advisory Council on Vocational Education. She is a former teacher and an international educational and psychological consultant. She has conducted workshops on group leadership training, career counseling and guidance, sex equity, and human relations in the United States, Europe, and Great Britain.